The Man Who Invented
Las Vegas

by
W.R. Wilkerson III

CIRO'S
BOOKS

Ciro's Books, in its commitment to preserving the written word, prints all its books on acid-free paper.

FIRST EDITION January 2000

ISBN 0-9676643-0-6

Library of Congress Registration No. TXu 588-357
Library of Congress Cataloging-in-Publication Data
Wilkerson III, W. R.
The Man Who Invented Las Vegas

Filing: 1. Title. 2. History of Las Vegas. 3. Biography.

Printed in the United States of America

For the late Tom Seward, my father's partner of fifteen years, and for my son who should know more about his grandfather.

Contents

Preface

I began compiling this record of my father, W. R. "Billy" Wilkerson in May 1972. It was then that my curiosity about him first bloomed. I interviewed all the principals on my father's side connected with the Flamingo, from his wives to business associates. I spent a great deal of time with the man who knew Billy Wilkerson best: George H. Kennedy, Jr. George began working for my father in 1933, first as his personal secretary and later as his general manager. He was also my godfather.

George retired from a life of faithful service to Billy Wilkerson shortly after his death in September 1962. From 1970 to a few months before his own death in 1991, George and I met regularly at his home in Ramona, California. I spent almost the entire month of August 1972 interviewing George in person or by phone. He talked freely and at length about my father. Unfortunately, while he did not object to being interviewed, George's aversion to being tape recorded made my job difficult.

In 1973 all the interviews (recorded from August to December 1972) stored at my family home were burglarized. Although I was initially disheartened, in one sense I felt the loss was not that great. George had been hinting about writing a book on my father for some time. I decided to wait for his book, and abandoned my project.

When George died in November 1991, it became my responsibility to tell my father's story. And so, once again, after nearly 20 years, and without George's help, I started from scratch.

In his 1991 book Little Man, British biographer Robert Lacey was the first to corroborate that the Flamingo's authorship rightfully belonged to Wilkerson, not Ben Siegel. When I contacted him, Robert gave me many helpful pointers. On his advice, for example, I steered clear of the gangster "boiler plate" and stayed exclusively with Wilkerson's story. So, as much as possible, the references to gangsters in this book are peripheral.

Few documents from this period have survived. This is particularly true of documents from the Nevada Project Corporation, the corporation belonging to Siegel and other organized crime figures involved in the Flamingo. Added to this, Wilkerson incinerated all his business and personal records from 1929 to 1950 in an office bonfire in 1951. The majority of this book then is based on the few documents that still exist and on firsthand accounts from those who worked for both Ben Siegel and Billy Wilkerson.

A thorough search of FBI files revealed little of value. Withheld, presumably, is the incriminating affidavit Greg Bautzer filed in the winter of 1946.

Many would not talk to me because of past ills Wilkerson had done to them. Gangsters associated with the Flamingo either did not want to talk with me at all, or quickly developed total amnesia despite the fact that their names appear on key documents.

At the onset of writing this book, two overriding questions concerned me. First, I struggled to find documentation directly linking Siegel to the vision of the hotel. This search was unsuccessful. Second, I questioned who could be credited for the invention of Las Vegas as it is known today. Although Tom Hull combined a hotel, casino and showroom under one roof in Las Vegas with the opening of his El Rancho Vegas in 1941, his vision was more "Western" than modern or European. Wilkerson devised an elegant American Monte Carlo for gamblers. With his Flamingo, the modern-day resort extravaganza arose in the desert.

In my early grammar school years we played a classroom game called, "Telephone." The teacher would whisper a single word in the first student's ear with instructions to pass it on to the next, until, one by one, row by row, the last student was obliged to reveal the secret. The word was never the same. At some point it became convoluted.

Myths are created in the same fashion. They spring to life the moment the truth is forgotten. They are further distorted by the permutations of the Telephone Game of History. As myths are passed on by word of mouth, they become universally accepted as truth. Myths also tend to elbow aside rightful claimants who remain silent.

Wilkerson's reluctance to openly claim authorship of the Flamingo during his lifetime encouraged history to forget him. He did not view the Flamingo as a particularly happy episode in his life. Wanting nothing more to do with the project, he did not take credit as the hotel's author following Siegel's death. After Wilkerson's departure in April 1947, he disassociated himself from the project, rarely mentioning it in public or private. History, of course, cordially accommodated his wishes by crediting the hotel to his arch nemesis and former pupil.

All too often, time itself adds its own problems to our

search for the truth. It is as if history suffers from Alzheimer's and like a sleeping Rip Van Winkle, must be awakened, or, in drastic cases like Wilkerson's, vigorously resuscitated. Along with the wholesale destruction of documents, books and entire libraries, inaccurate reporting also adds to history's shortcomings. Less than rigorous news reports create the perfect breeding ground for myths. Simply put, a lack of vigilance regarding the truth allows the facts to disappear and myths to emerge. Equally disturbing, it is extremely difficult to stem this re-writing of history, especially in the wake of powerful feature films.

To date, history has failed Wilkerson. He is the quintessential victim of myth. During his lifetime, Wilkerson enjoyed enormous celebrity status. For three decades, practically everyone in Hollywood knew him, or of him. Yet a mere thirty years after his death Billy Wilkerson is practically unknown.

As George Kennedy said, "History is the last man at the typewriter."

W. R. Wilkerson III
March 1995

1. The Man

Billy Wilkerson took Hollywood by storm in 1930. The suave, swashbuckling impresario remained a dominant influence in the film industry for the next three decades.

Wilkerson's movie connections began humbly in 1916 with a Nickelodeon. He was away from home, studying medicine in Philadelphia, when his father, a renowned gambler, died unexpectedly leaving behind a mountain of debts. Young Wilkerson was forced to find employment to support himself and his mother.

Two weeks later, on a World Series bet, a friend from medical school won a movie theater located in Fort Lee, New Jersey. Wilkerson agreed to manage the tiny Nickelodeon in exchange for half the profits.

Wilkerson found the fledgling film industry very much to his liking. Between 1918 and 1929 he held an assortment of movie jobs ranging from film sales to producing one-reelers for a small picture company. For a spell he was also District Manager at Universal Pictures under Karl Laemmle.[1] By 1929 he had acquired a partnership in a Manhattan trade paper devoted to the film business.[2] Realizing the limitations of a New York base, Wilkerson began dreaming of starting the first daily trade paper for

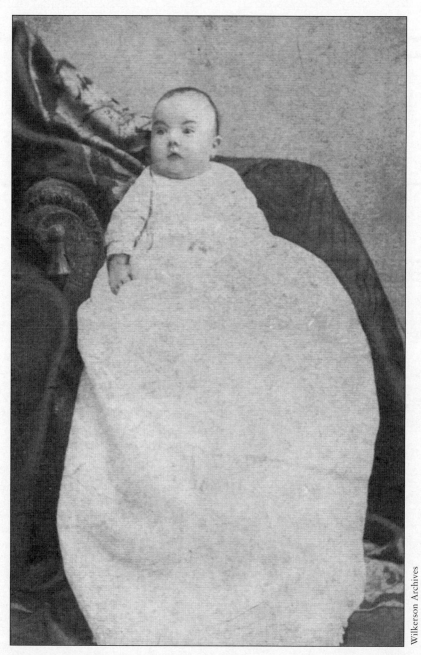

Wilkerson at nine months old. Tennessee, 1891.

Wilkerson at medical school. Philadelphia, 1912.

the motion picture industry in the place where the movies were being made — out west, in Hollywood. This dream would become his life's work.

It began as a riches-to-rags story. In late October 1929, he bumped into a Wall Street chum who "advised him to play the Market at rock bottom".[3] Wilkerson sold his half-interest in the Manhattan trade paper for $20,000 and borrowed an additional $25,000. On "Black Tuesday", October 29, Wilkerson's thirty-ninth birthday, he walked into the Wall Street Stock Exchange at ten in the morning with the intention of doubling his money and hightailing it to California. Forty-five minutes later the market crashed and a dazed Wilkerson wandered out of the building without a dime to his name.[4]

Undaunted, he packed his wife, his mother and their few belongings into a dilapidated flivver and motored cross-country to Hollywood. There, on July 26, 1930, he formed the Wilkerson Daily Corporation and on September 3, 1930 the first issue of The Hollywood Reporter rolled off the presses.

This daily magazine reported on movies, studios and personalities in an outrageously candid style. Through its outspoken pages Wilkerson became one of the town's most colorful and controversial figures. He was Hollywood's champion and conscience, its loudest critic and most vehement booster. His opinions reflected the turbulent times and mercurial moods of the town's famed Golden Era.

But the first six years were anything but easy for Wilkerson. The Reporter did not receive an enthusiastic reception. The country was, after all, awash in the Great Depression. To make matters worse, Hollywood was a company town ruthlessly controlled by a handful of autonomous, iron-fisted studio heads. Men like Louis B. Mayer and Harry Cohn were used to being obeyed, not admonished. A bad movie review or an outspoken editorial could lead to a studio withdrawing valuable advertising support for months at a time. Wilkerson fought back, hacking at the studio heads with his typewriter. He began each issue with a stinging self-penned editorial entitled "Tradeviews," which exposed corrupt studio practices and launched an all-out attack on the studio system in general. The upstart publisher also employed hard-ball tactics to solicit advertising. Studios were literally blackmailed into giving their support. If they refused, he ordered a complete editorial blackout on all their material – from press releases to film reviews.

Wilkerson with his editorial staff. Hollywood, 1936.

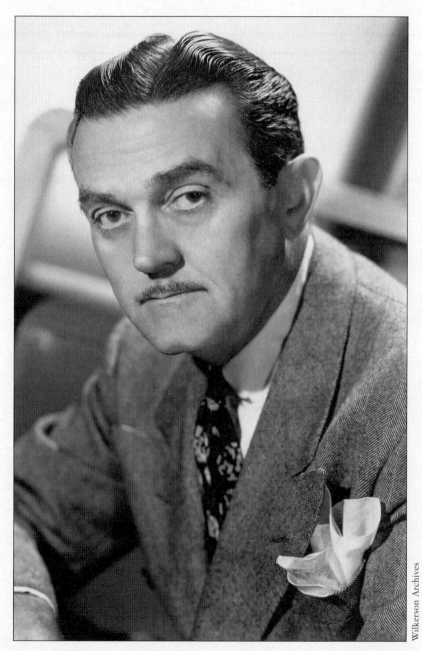

Studio photo of Wilkerson. Hollywood, 1945.

During lean periods, Wilkerson knew how to man the machinery himself. Hollywood, 1936.

The corporate moguls eventually banded together to deal with The Reporter. They refused Wilkerson all advertising support and deprived him of news from their studios. They even hired extra employees to burn The Hollywood Reporter when it was delivered every morning at their front gates.

At the height of the battle, his reporters were barred from every lot in town. Wilkerson told them to climb over studio walls and sift through the executives' garbage. These tactics produced a flood of incriminating news, which Wilkerson cheerfully printed.

Many times Wilkerson was on the verge of closing down his operation only to be bailed out by loans from friends such as Joseph Schenck or Howard Hughes. Eventually, his dogged perseverance won the day.

Wilkerson Archives

Hard at work. Hollywood, 1936

"Tradeviews" became one of the most widely read daily columns in the industry. The Reporter, by now fondly referred to as "the industry's Bible," gained national prominence. Even President Franklin D. Roosevelt had the paper airmailed daily to his desk at the White House. By 1936, The Hollywood Reporter had become something even the most prescient studio heads had never anticipated – a power that rivaled their own.

But Wilkerson wasn't content with establishing himself as a magazine publisher. He wanted to become a night club proprietor as well. There were, in his opinion, two very good reasons for launching new ventures in Hollywood at the onset of the Great Depression. Judged by his standards, existing venues were "pedestrian." They lacked ambiance, glamor and sophistication. The second and most compelling reason was that people in the entertainment industry had money to spend – lots of it.

The inspiration for these Hollywood ventures came from his New York speakeasy triumphs during the Prohibition 1920s, and his many trips to Europe. Wilkerson's beloved Parisian nightspots became the model for a string of highly profitable nightclubs, cafes and restaurants.

While the movie industry dominated the town, Hollywood's social center was the fabled Sunset Strip, where stars went to see and be seen. Wilkerson's nightspots – Vendome, Cafe Trocadero, Sunset House, Ciro's, LaRue, and L'Aiglon – contributed much to the Golden Era's dazzling glamor. During this magical time, Wilkerson became the nation's most successful restaurant and nightclub impresario.

Wilkerson Archives

*Hob-nobbing with patron Cary Grant at Cafe Trocadero.
Hollywood, 1934.*

The publisher preferred the suave and swanky to the colloquial. His tastes were distinctly European, rather than American.

"He brought Paris to Hollywood," film director Joe Pasternak fondly remembered, "at a time when Hollywood was still eating sandwiches and drinking Coca Colas."[5]

These Hollywood landmarks were to lay the groundwork for his most ambitious venture in the Las Vegas desert.

But the rambunctious, often ruthless visionary with the Midas touch was not without enemies. Wilkerson was as much hated as he was loved, as much a thorn in the side of

Hollywood as he was lionized. He was credited with the discovery of such screen legends as Lana Turner, but he destroyed just as many prominent careers. While he championed the cause of labor in Hollywood in the early 1930s, in the late 1940s he brought the industry to task for communism.

If Wilkerson's business life was turbulent, his domestic life was no better. A stubborn, driven man, he let nothing stand in his way when it came to profits. He was an insufferable workaholic, and he paid for his success with five failed marriages and poor health. As his second wife Edith Gwynn explained shortly after their divorce, "Billy's real mistress is his work."[6]

Being married to the overbearing publisher drove several of his wives to alcoholism. "He treated his wives like possessions," recalled fifth wife, Vivian Du Bois. "We were bookends on a mantelpiece, that's all."[7]

Above all, Wilkerson was a man riddled with paradoxes and contradictions. While he was the proprietor of some of Hollywood's greatest restaurants, cafes, and nightclubs, at home he usually dined on canned sardines on toast and deviled-egg sandwiches. And, despite five divorces, he remained a devout Roman Catholic his entire life.

Despite his high-profile profession, Wilkerson shunned the light of personal publicity. He was a private man, even a loner, and he preferred the company of his beloved French poodles to any wife or friend.

In every facet and area of his life the man was compulsive. Sitting at his desk, for example, he could consume an average of twenty Cokes and three packs of cigarettes daily. But just like his father before him, Wilkerson's greatest weakness by far was gambling. A lifelong "compulsive gambler" long before the term was coined, he regularly risked vast sums of money on the roll of dice. In the first six months of 1944, for example, he gambled away almost $1 million, and came perilously close to bankruptcy. Joseph Schenck, then chairman of 20th Century Fox Pictures and a personal friend of Wilkerson's, told him: "If you are going to gamble that kind of money, own the Casa."[8]

2. The Gambling Bug

Wilkerson inherited his obsessive and dangerous passion for gambling from his father, William Richard "Big Dick" Wilkerson, who was a gambler by trade. Big Dick died penniless, but he was something of a folk hero in the Old South. He made gambling history in 1902 when, on the turn of a card in a poker game, he won the Coca Cola concession and bottling rights for 13 southern states. Dick quickly traded these rights for a movie theater which he sold two weeks later, and raised $4,000.[1] Almost as soon as he got the cash in hand, Dick risked and lost it in another poker game.[2]

Wilkerson Sr.'s gambling made for a turbulent domestic life. His wife Mary recalled that one day they would be the proud owners of a large cotton plantation with dozens of field workers, and the next they would be out in the same fields picking cotton for someone else.[3]

Like his father, Wilkerson was bitten by the gambling bug early. The origins of this destructive addiction can be traced to an overbearing mother, his gambling, alcoholic father, and a generally unhappy childhood.[4] Games of chance became young Wilkerson's much-needed escape from this oppression, and later, from his own personal woes and rocky domestic life.

While attending medical school in the early 1900s, he began betting on the World Series and the track. Card games quickly followed. He gambled wherever he could – on ships, trains and later even on planes. His addiction took him to the tables and race courses of the world, and eventually to Monte Carlo, where fortunes were won and lost in a single evening. The more he lost, the more determined he became to win his money back. He was so unwilling to accept his losses that he often accused fellow players of cheating.

"Playing poker with Billy was dangerous," according to film director Raoul Walsh, one of Wilkerson's many card-

Wilkerson at the races. Los Angeles, 1945.

playing friends. "He was a terrible card player and a sore loser."[5]

From the moment Wilkerson awoke in the morning he thought of nothing else but gambling. It consumed him. He planned his entire day around the gaming tables and race courses. Usually he would work in the morning and head out for the track in the afternoon.

Whenever possible, Wilkerson gambled every day. In Hollywood, he paid regular afternoon visits to Santa Anita or Hollywood Park. He kept a pair of dice in his coat pocket, and a deck of playing cards was never far from reach. At restaurants he would roll the dice on tabletops to determine who picked up the check. Even in his own restaurants, guests paid if they lost.[6]

Until the late 1930s, Hollywood was wide open to gambling and prostitution, but when California outlawed these activities, compulsive gamblers like Wilkerson were forced to travel out of state in search of legal gambling. This frequently meant long, daunting drives across searing deserts and snow-covered mountains or lurching water-taxi rides to gaming ships moored outside U.S. waters.

Las Vegas, Nevada was a favorite gambling spot of Wilkerson's. He would charter a plane in the morning from Los Angeles Municipal Airport, and after a short cab ride he'd be inside a casino. He would then spend a few hours at the tables, making or losing between ten to twenty thousand dollars before returning to Hollywood. If he was particularly unlucky he would play through the night hoping for his luck to change, and fly back the following morning.[7]

Wilkerson would frequently drive down to Agua Caliente, a sprawling gambling facility on the Mexican border which was popular with the Hollywood movie colony. This enormous establishment offered everything from the complete range of table games to racetrack betting. He would spend the entire day there, lose twelve or fifteen thousand dollars, and then drive back again.

"He was in seventh heaven in Caliente," remembered Walsh. "If he didn't have enough of that," Walsh added, "he'd stay at night for the dog racing."[8]

Like most compulsive gamblers, Wilkerson played for the seductive lure of winning big money easily and quickly. Yet there was more to it than the something-for-nothing ethos of casino gaming. For Wilkerson, gambling represented a rush that rivaled any sexual experience.

Most chronic gamblers are superstitious. Wilkerson was no exception. An ardent Catholic, he relied heavily on prayer and a lucky rabbit's foot on his key chain that had gone bald from rubbing. He would stand by the table with his eyes closed, clutching the rabbit's foot and whispering Hail Marys as he rolled the dice.

Wilkerson had three main loves in the world of gambling: craps, poker and the track. He rarely missed the legendary private poker games that were held weekly at Samuel Goldywn's or Joe Schenck's house. These games were played with $20,000 chips, and Wilkerson regularly lost thousands a visit.

"You had to be rich to gamble that kind of cash at those games," recalled Tom Seward, Wilkerson's business partner for fifteen years.[9] "Only the biggies would be there."

An invitation to these all-night, no-limit games clearly signaled one's arrival into the highest echelons of

Hollywood. They attracted such notables as Sid Grauman, Darryl Zanuck, Charles Skouras, Jack Warner, Irving Thalberg, Carl "Junior" Laemmle, and David O. Selznick. Even Irving Berlin regularly played cards in this august company. Wilkerson often hosted his own discreet back room card games at the restaurants he controlled. The well-heeled attendees were hand-picked from Hollywood's power elite.[10]

Although he never publicly acknowledged his gambling, Wilkerson's vice was no secret to those who knew and worked for him. Most Fridays he would take the business payroll and stake it all at a local horse racetrack. He was even known to risk the Reporter's prepaid advertising receipts. This gambling was tolerated by his loyal employees who often overlooked their employer's excesses – and even took occasional temporary pay cuts to cover his losses.

George Kennedy, the publisher's personal secretary and general manager for more than three decades, saw Wilkerson through every phase of his meteoric career. He was also privy to the publisher's tragic weaknesses and dramatic downfalls.[11] Kennedy remembered that the Bank of America in Hollywood would often call him to ask which obligations it should honor first – the payroll or Wilkerson's gambling debts.[12]

Under the guise of business, Wilkerson often disappeared to Las Vegas on gambling sprees that lasted for days at a time. With the sole exception of his general manager and business partner, the publisher's whereabouts during such trips were kept secret.

If his luck ran out at the tables, Wilkerson would phone Hollywood and instruct Kennedy to go to the bank. The faithful general manager would collect an attaché case from the branch manager and take the first flight to Las Vegas. There he would hand over the case to his employer.

"I lost count of how many cases I delivered to Mr. Wilkerson," said Kennedy. "And I knew I wasn't carrying Christmas cards."[13]

These "shipments" sometimes contained as much as $50,000 in cash.[14]

After handing over the case, Kennedy would be summarily sent back to Hollywood.

"If I arrived in Las Vegas late at night, I would have to camp out on a desk top in the manager's office until I could catch the early flight back."[15]

When Wilkerson couldn't get hold of ready cash, he would write IOUs – scores of them. He penned these promissory notes on whatever came to hand – scraps of paper, table napkins, anything – so long as his eyes never had to leave the table. Casino owners regularly gave him extraordinary lines of credit. because they knew that he was good for it. Whatever the amount wagered and lost, Wilkerson had a reputation for honoring his gambling debts. Wilkerson's sometimes daily IOUs, "customer's" and racetrack "cage" checks never totaled less than $500 a day, and at times they escalated as high as $27,000.

Kennedy remembered receiving frantic phone calls from the bank, asking for signature verification on these questionable documents.

"They used to drive the bank crazy," Kennedy said. "They would go nuts trying to figure out what these doilies with large dollar amounts written on them were."[16]

On one occasion the branch manager called Wilkerson's office to verify an IOU for $23,750 that appeared to be written on toilet paper. Kennedy asked if the document bore Wilkerson's signature. The branch manager confirmed that it did. Kennedy reluctantly replied, "Well, I guess you'd better honor it then."[17]

Wilkerson would acquire large sums of money quickly and then gamble them away with equal speed. In 1936 he decided to purchase a small hotel on the French Riviera near Monte Carlo. The idea was to acquire property near a legal gambling region. He borrowed the $75,000 he needed from his friend Joe Schenck, and flew to the south of France. Two weeks later he telephoned Schenck and confessed that he had gone straight to the casino at Monte Carlo and had lost the entire amount within two days.[18]

Friends often bailed the publisher out with timely loans, which yanked him back from the brink of bankruptcy. Sometimes Wilkerson's mother, Mary, was his rescuer. He never kept secrets from her, and he told her about his gambling losses in spite of the discomfort he knew such disclosures caused her. He always made sure that she had funds, because he didn't want her to endure the same misery she had experienced with his father.

Mary was a frugal woman with a deep distrust of banks that harked back to the years when her husband had been refused financial assistance by them. She squirreled away the money her son gave her into empty coffee cans that she stored next to her sugar and spices. On four separate occasions, Wilkerson's mother came to his rescue after he had gambled away the company payroll – but she never let him leave without a good scolding.[19]

Wilkerson's enormous talent for creating successful businesses was almost perfectly balanced by his willingness to risk everything on the turn of a card. He pursued his obsession with the same tireless zeal, and generally with the same disastrous results, as his father. The only difference was that Wilkerson labored almost an entire lifetime to subsidize his gambling. He was fortunately possessed with a psychological resilience that allowed him to weather staggering losses, and while he often had money to squander, those who knew him were amazed that he managed to avoid bankruptcy. Even in a good year he never lost less than $150,000.

But all this would change in November of 1944. Wilkerson, like his father before him, was about to step into the pages of gambling history. The compulsion that ruled him so completely was to inspire the largest, most ambitious facility that gambling had ever seen.

3. The Idea

1944 was shaping up as a horrendous year for Billy Wilkerson. His gambling at the tables and racecourses had cost him dearly.[1] By July his losses neared the $750,000 mark and associates were predicting that he would easily surpass that figure by the end of the year.

Wilkerson could gamble such enormous sums away because of three thriving businesses he owned. Two were restaurants, LaRue and Ciro's. The third was The Hollywood Reporter. The trio grossed just over $1 million in revenues a year.[2] After he deducted the total expenses and operating costs of his businesses, he was left with around $250,000 a year. A prudent man would have set this profit aside for emergencies or investment funds, but Wilkerson didn't think like that.[3]

"A chronic gambler does not keep ready supplies of cash within reach," George Kennedy remembered. "Because Mr. Wilkerson was a heavy gambler there was little in the way of cash reserves in the bank, at least nothing approaching the figures he was gambling."[4]

Since Wilkerson had few, if any, personal expenses he could afford to lose large sums of cash. To him it was petty cash, disposable income. He had no overhead in terms of food bills. He always dined in luxury at his own restaurants.

Wilkerson also had no entertainment expenses. By 1944, the studios were eagerly pursuing the publisher to personally view their new releases. More often than not, a studio would provide him and his guests with a private screening room on the lot. One studio chairman went so far as to supply him with screening facilities and a projectionist in his own home.[5]

The studios were keenly aware of Wilkerson's lavish personal tastes. He was known in the industry as a man who exemplified class through his restaurants, and lifestyle. The suave, dapper dresser personified the finer things in life, cultivating a waxed mustache and often visiting his restaurants in tails and spats. He wore elegant clothes from London and drove expensive cars.

This lifestyle was born out of a personal promise exacted from himself. After his father's death he vowed that neither he nor his mother would ever again feel the sting of poverty. As a loving, faithful son, Wilkerson worked hard to fulfill that promise. The problem, of course, resided in the gambling compulsion which had dogged him since his youth. Yet no matter how bad things got, his determination to preserve the lifestyle he had designed for himself steered him away from the jaws of destitution.

A steady stream of generous gifts – from large tins of Beluga Caviar (a favorite of Wilkerson's) to season baseball tickets – flowed into his office year-round from those interested in courting the publisher's favor. Nor did Wilkerson's love affair with long distance travel go unnoticed. The studios catered to his love of travel by flying him first class across the country for film junkets. Studio limos met him at airports around the globe and film companies regularly picked up the tab for his travel and accommodations. At times, even his clothing and cars were complimentary.[6]

Since he owed no money, Wilkerson enjoyed an excellent credit rating at the Bank of America, which he rarely used. As a rule of thumb, he avoided bank loans like an infectious rash. When he needed cash for a new project, old friends like Howard Hughes or Joe Schenck would advance him funds under the guise of pre-paid advertising.

Much to his business advisors' despair, Wilkerson hated investing money in established businesses. He funded expansion sparingly and only rarely bought real-estate. The land his restaurants sat upon was always leased, not owned.

But the publisher's most disconcerting business practice was his habit of selling out ventures, like his restaurants, at the height of their popularity and success on what often appeared to be pure whims, devoid of any sound judgment. When close friends, puzzled by this behavior, questioned his logic, Wilkerson bluntly replied, "I'm bored with it." The sweet taste of success quickly palled after its initial intoxication, so selling his businesses at their apex made perfect sense to the publisher. He was rarely content, and he spent his life restlessly pursuing new victories.

The publisher's personal extravagance did not go unnoticed by his mother, Mary, whose strict Catholic upbringing espoused self-denial. Although she lived well, few ever recall her indulging herself financially. She had hoped that this frugal philosophy would somehow rub off on her son. It was not to be. To Mary's dismay, her son enjoyed showering his many wives with lavish gifts almost as much as he loved his gambling.

Losing vast sums at the tables and tracks always increased Wilkerson's resolve to either win or earn back the money he had lost. After he'd lost he would re-double his money and efforts and gamble more fiercely than before, usually with disastrous results.

At other times, he would become filled with self-loathing and furiously apply himself to his work. In either case, wives, friends, co-workers and associates all found him insufferable after an unsuccessful gambling expedition.

"He was always bitchy after returning from a bad stint in Vegas," remembered George Kennedy. "People around the office became the brunt of his disappointment and anger. I was one. But we all took it in stride and after a few days he was back to normal."

By 1944, Wilkerson was far from stepping back from the gaming tables. Before March he had devoured the Reporter's annual profit and by July was already biting into a substantial portion of his gross receipts. Despite owning three immensely successful businesses, Wilkerson found himself almost broke. The lurking specter of bankruptcy loomed over him.

To those within the ranks of his organization privy to these numbers, the losses were daunting. They felt that it was only a matter of time before gambling succeeded in crippling both Wilkerson and his businesses.[7]

Wilkerson's gambling also took its toll on many relationships from marriages to partnerships.

"I watched Billy gamble my future away," said Tom Seward, who sued the publisher for corporate mismanagement in 1951.

Even close colleagues, grudgingly accepting of his habit

in the past, began to think that their employer was going over the edge. They saw their livelihoods being tossed recklessly onto the crap table. Adding to their understandable frustration was the publisher's blindness towards his mania. His stubborn, macho denial of the problem offered them little hope that he would ever quit of his own volition.

In addition, a second obstacle threatened Wilkerson's delicately balanced finances. A societal acceptance of gambling pervaded Hollywood, much as it had Europe for centuries. Gambling debts in particular garnered a unique status. They were an accepted part of the town's culture, much like dueling scars were in Germany up until the late 1920s. The greater the amounts wagered and lost, the more prestige attached to the loser.

As George Kennedy explained, "The mere fact that you could afford to blow that kind of cash indicated in some way that you were a mover and a shaker."[8]

This easy tolerance of gambling hampered Wilkerson's attempts to control his costly addiction. By fall 1944, the first prediction his associates had made came to pass. Wilkerson's gambling debts crested the $1 million mark. But ever at a fever pitch, he relentlessly gambled on, wagering every penny he could raise.

"We all held our breath," remembered Kennedy. "I went to Mass every morning and prayed."[9]

That September the second prediction grimly materialized. The situation went from bad to worse when Wilkerson was unable to pay important business bills. One after another, major vendors halted shipments of paper, ink, etc. Those goods which did arrive, came COD. Lacking operating funds, the publisher faced his most severe business challenge to date.

In addition to putting a strain on his business finances, Wilkerson's gambling had also forced him into ethically compromising situations. If he was unable to pay his gambling markers at the weekly high-stakes, no-limit poker games with Hollywood's movie brass, he would barter away his advertising.[10] Debts to Joe Schenck, however, were forgiven by the movie tycoon.[11]

On the personal front, Wilkerson's gambling fever was also approaching its final, seemingly-inevitable crescendo. By November, the financial beatings simply became too painful for even Wilkerson to ignore and he finally woke up to the monstrosity of his disease.[12]

He had been working hard ever since his father's death to support a chronic gambling addiction, and he felt isolated in his newfound awareness. There was little practical or professional help available to him at that time. There were, as yet, no organizations devoted to treating compulsive gamblers. The afflicted had to fend for themselves.

Wilkerson, at long last, began viewing gambling as an affliction rather than a hobby. He searched avidly for a cure.[13] In late November, the publisher poured his heart out to Joe Schenck over a quiet dinner alone at the movie tycoon's home. Schenck listened sympathetically as Wilkerson admitted his problem. The mogul was quick to offer the beleaguered publisher a fatherly piece of advice: "Be on the other side of the table if you are going to suffer those kinds of losses." When Wilkerson asked what he meant, Schenck added, "Build a casino. Own the house."[14]

The suggestion carried great weight because it came

Billy Wilkerson, Joe Schenck and Greg Bautzer.
Hollywood, 1952.

from Schenck, who was himself a chronic gambler and had suffered heavy losses. Wilkerson pondered this friendly advice for days. As far back as 1933 he had toyed with the idea of starting a gambling place. At that time, however, it had seemed unnecessary. Before the gambling crackdown of 1938, Hollywood was wide open for gambling and prostitution. Clubs like the Clover and the Colony offered local gamblers well-oiled operations in their own back yards.[15]

If that failed to tickle the gambler's fancy, there were always the gambling ships. Moored off the Santa Monica coast, floating casinos, like The Rex and The S.S. Tango, had operated legally outside the United States territorial three-mile limit since 1929, providing as sophisticated a gambling operation as any found on dry land.[16] Southern California also had several race tracks.[17]

Wilkerson saw no reason to add to this wide variety. Instead he concentrated on creating high-class, entertainment-oriented restaurants and nightclubs, capable of attracting the town's elite. In 1938 however, all gambling and prostitution in Hollywood was shut down. The following year, the new attorney general of California, Earl Warren, also outlawed all oceangoing gambling off the California coastline. By 1940, legal gambling in California was restricted to the horse racing tracks. Wilkerson witnessed these closures with dismay and frustration. He, like many others, began a search for alternate venues.

Joe Schenck and William Paley, who was then the head of Columbia Broadcasting, jointly represented a consortium of investors in the Arrowhead Springs Hotel in Lake Arrowhead, California. This remote hotel, located in the mountains more than three hours from Hollywood, had been losing money for years. Because of Wilkerson's many successful clubs and restaurants, Schenck asked him to come to the hotel's rescue. He wanted Wilkerson to serve as the hotel's consulting manager and make the floundering enterprise profitable.

At first, Wilkerson did not consider the Arrowhead Springs much of a business opportunity. He viewed its prospects as limited. Most of his friends and business associates shared this view. Furthermore, they did not understand why he would want to involve himself with something outside Hollywood. But the real reason for renovating the hotel was not immediately apparent to outsiders.

Wilkerson had always been grateful to Schenck. He was the one studio mogul who had steadfastly supported the publisher when all the other studios had turned against him. During lean periods, Schenck could be counted on to advance enough pre-paid advertising to keep The Reporter solvent. Wilkerson was only too happy to return his friend's favor.[18]

Wilkerson agreed to accept the offer on the condition that he was allowed to lease the hotel with an option to buy. As an owner-operator himself he was used to making all creative calls without interference. He would be in a much better position to turn the hotel around if he had this freedom.[19] Wilkerson also suggested a one year time limit. If he proved successful, he could exercise his option and take over the hotel. Eager to see their business succeed, the two men gladly gave Wilkerson a contract. In November 1940, Wilkerson leased the six-story hotel for a year.[20]

The publisher began by improving the restaurant. He replaced the staff with the finest help he could import from Hollywood. He added gala functions and parties and upgraded the menu. Heavy advertising in The Reporter boosted visitors by extolling the mountain's scenic virtues and champagne breezes. An awed Paley and Schenck watched in amazement as patrons began flooding in through their doors. Within a few months the hotel was in the black for the first time in years.

Whether Wilkerson initially saw the Arrowhead Springs as a gambling opportunity or this idea evolved with the hotel's increasing success is not known. Once the venue became popular, however, he began risking a few infrequent backroom card games. A carefully hand-picked clientele guaranteed maximum discretion.[21]

News of the illicit card games quickly spread. In Hollywood scores of regular patrons who had been missing their pastime since the 1938 crackdown flocked to the mountain retreat. The hotel's very remoteness helped lull these gamblers into a false sense of security. A weekend of relaxation in the fresh mountain air, an evening of fine dining and entertainment followed by a quiet card game and a comfortable hotel bed proved an irresistible lure for the publisher's Hollywood friends.

Wilkerson could not have predicted the runaway popularity of these games. Caught totally by surprise, he soon found himself unable to keep up with the demand. Although a dedicated gambler, he knew little about gaming mechanics or management. Wilkerson contacted some acquaintances who had been responsible for gambling operations at The Clover Club in Hollywood.[22] These men were made partners in the Arrowhead Springs gambling operation for a percentage of the take, thus freeing the publisher to concentrate on running the hotel.[23]

Soon the gaming operation was expanded. The rear of the hotel facing the mountain became a private area with a full complement of tables and other gambling equipment. Finally, Wilkerson had his gambling facility. And a highly successful one at that.

Unfortunately, his happiness was short-lived. The appealing isolation of the location backfired when Lake Arrowhead authorities became aware that the Springs was being used for gambling. In May 1940 they decided to make their move. A mounted posse of U.S. marshals rode down the mountain at the hotel's rear. During the raid, tables were overturned and gambling equipment smashed by zealous deputies wielding axes. The marshals closed the hotel down.[24]

With the Arrowhead Springs gone, Wilkerson tried to forget Schenck's advice. Yet four years later his friend's throwaway comment about owning the table rekindled new enthusiasm. The idea appealed to Wilkerson for two major reasons. First, he could have control over his own place. This had always been important to him. He firmly believed that success in any venture hinged on establishing total control over every aspect of the operation. Equally important, by the close of 1944, his compulsion was completely out of control and he desperately needed a gambling outlet.

Just what form this venture should take and where it should be located were still uncertain to him. His primary requirement was that the gambling had to be legal. Although, thanks to the publisher's numerous Hollywood contacts, the Arrowhead Springs bust hadn't led to formal charges being filed against him, the publisher had had more than his fill of illegal gaming.

Wilkerson began researching possible gambling locations. For a time he considered breeding thoroughbred horses to compete at the local tracks in Southern California. Although Wilkerson loved the track, he eventually rejected this idea as too risky. He knew little about thoroughbred breeding and training. To make matters worse, bets at the tracks were often fixed.[24]

He briefly flirted with an operation in Cuba. There were definite benefits to setting up shop there, the two most enticing attractions being legal gambling and tax-free profits so long as the income remained undeclared in the U.S., However Cuba was a long way from Beverly Hills and doing business under a foreign flag could be risky.

Wilkerson had hoped to find a choice of possible gaming locations dotting the U.S. map. Much to his dismay, only one state in the Union could boast legal casino gambling in 1944: Nevada. Although the Silver State initially met his prerequisites for quiet remoteness within reach of Hollywood, it also presented numerous drawbacks. The terrain was harsh, and the weather even harsher. Temperatures frequently soared passed the century mark or plunged below freezing. Yet Nevada's sun-blasted wastelands and snow-covered landscapes possessed one unique and, to Wilkerson, irresistible asset – legalized casino gambling within the United States.

Gambling's rocky road had led him to the wasteland that was the Nevada desert in search of an answer to his horrific disorder.

4. The Vision

Gambling had been legal in Nevada since 1931, but most of the activity was centered around Reno and Carson City – the state capital in the north. Wilkerson fixed his sights on Las Vegas, a small but ambitious town some five hundred miles south of Reno.

Up until 1940, Las Vegas consisted primarily of a few blocks of small rustic hotels decorated in a charming dude ranch motif and a series of casinos affectionately known as "gambling halls" or "gambling shacks," occupying Second and Fremont.[1] A departure from these hotels came with Tom Hull's El Rancho Vegas in 1941, which, as the first hotel-casino-showroom combination, ushered in a new era. The town, energized by a booming wartime economy, was poised to welcome defense workers and soldiers. Because of this influx, there were ten hotels and thirteen casinos lit with neon by 1945.

Wilkerson had frequented the town since the construction of Boulder Dam in the early 1930s had ensured its fresh water supply. He enjoyed the variety of gambling Las Vegas offered. With a myriad of choices at his disposal, Wilkerson happily roamed from one casino to another. If his luck was down at one casino, he simply moved on to the next. "When I feel the table turn cold," he once said, "I leave the casino."[2]

Wilkerson's Las Vegas Customer Checks for April 5, 1945.

34

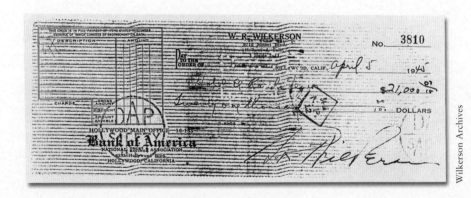

Wilkerson's Las Vegas Customer Checks for April 5, 1945.

Wilkerson's gambling losses on a fairly typical Las Vegas gambling day (April 5th, 1945) were as follows:

Hotel Last Frontier	$825.00
S. S. Rex Club	$3,025.00
Hotel El Rancho	$21,000.00
Pioneer Club	$900.00
	$25,750.00

It is important to mention that Wilkerson had some astonishing wins on occasion, but these gains were quickly devoured by the gaming tables.

In December 1944, Wilkerson attempted to stem his gambling losses by leasing the El Rancho Vegas from then-owner Joe Drown for six months.[3] Wilkerson paid Drown $50,000 for the six month lease. But even then the publisher had greater ambitions. He knew that if he were to build in Nevada, he would need something much grander and larger in scale than he originally envisioned or had previously created in Hollywood – something that would accommodate far more than just a casino. He shrewdly sensed that no matter how magnificent the casino, Las Vegas would remain a hard sell to the snobbish movie crowd back home. Something fantastic would be needed to tempt Beverly Hills gamblers into crossing the desert.

In 1944, his crisis forced the publisher to take a more serious look at Las Vegas. Wilkerson's initial enthusiasm paled as he studied the town in more detail. He concluded that Las Vegas suited only diehard gamblers like himself. Even Wilkerson, who loved gambling, hated the desert. It was the complete antithesis of his beloved Mediterranean. The rustic Western-style casinos and hotels were not Beverly Hills or Monte Carlo. There were no elegant cafes and a distinct lack of high-society night life. In short, Las Vegas lacked the distinctive elements of glamor and sophistication that Wilkerson had enjoyed in other places around the globe. In addition to this, there was no escape from the unrelenting heat and the unsightly desert terrain. At night Wilkerson slept poorly. It was an example of just how far he would go to indulge his addiction.

In the past Wilkerson's obsession had blinded him to the unsightliness of the town, which was ironic for a man who prided himself on his exquisite taste, and who crafted fine dining and entertainment experiences with the skill of a virtuoso violinist – a man who dressed immaculately every day of his life and whose lifestyle included frequenting the playgrounds of the rich. But until then he had not viewed gambling in America as the elegant vacation experience it was in Europe.

But he was led by the same desires that lure every gambler to the felt tables – the dream of easy money.

To him, Las Vegas lacked almost all the ingredients, such as breathtaking scenery and good weather, that were needed to guarantee success. Apart from legal prostitution, the town provided little to tempt gamblers to remain there with their winnings.

Yet, in the end, the town's very remoteness and isolation helped convinced the publisher that Las Vegas could become an ideal gambling location. Once there, visitors would be free of other distractions, as they had been in the seclusion of the Arrowhead Springs. Far from any metropolis, they would spend more time placing wagers.

After Wilkerson re-examined the assets of the town he also realized there was a huge potential market for Las

Vegas in Hollywood. Hundreds of people like himself were eager to indulge their pastime if they could gamble legally and without major inconvenience.

The question of getting to Las Vegas remained. Wilkerson had always made the trip to Las Vegas exclusively by plane. While he preferred to fly, he knew most of his upscale Hollywood and Beverly Hills clientele enjoyed driving. A research trip seemed in order.

In January 1945, Wilkerson loaded extra gas cans into his Cadillac's trunk and set out across California's Mojave Desert to see for himself. He took Route 66 out of Los Angeles, and passed through Pasadena, San Bernardino, Victorville and Barstow. When he left Barstow, the publisher turned onto Route 91, and passed through Baker, California. He drove through hot, seemingly endless deserts and relentless, searing heat. This was the sun's anvil, a lunar landscape, an almost unendurable inferno. With air-conditioning in cars still a distant mirage, the dust-ridden drive was excruciatingly hot. The desolate highway was empty of gas stations and rest areas. Described by some as the last frontier, the drive to Las Vegas still echoed the Old West, lost in heat waves, sagebrush and the fathomless slumber of time.

Seven hours after leaving Los Angeles and some 300 hot desert miles later, Wilkerson coasted into Las Vegas – the closest legalized gambling location to Beverly Hills. Clearly, he felt, it would be asking too much to expect highbrow Hollywood patrons to leave their cozy private card games to brave an arduous drive in grueling weather only to face accommodations and amenities that were, by his standards, totally inadequate.

Although the vision for this irresistible attraction was still unformed at this point, he knew that it required a sizable piece of land. On a taxi ride from the El Rancho Vegas to the small Las Vegas airport with partner Tom Seward in late January 1945, Wilkerson spotted a For Sale sign on a large parcel of land. Two dilapidated shacks and a crumbling motel sign occupied a corner of the lot. There was a phone number on the sign. "Take that number down," Wilkerson barked at Seward.[4] It didn't matter that the land was situated several miles out of town.

Wilkerson learned that the thirty-three-acre lot belonged to Margaret M. Folsom, a small hotel owner who was down on her luck. He contacted his attorney, Greg Bautzer – a handsome playboy lawyer who had bedded many of Hollywood's most prominent stars and starlets, including Joan Crawford and the young Lana Turner. The Hollywood socialite attorney often cemented his deals over dinner at Wilkerson's clubs and restaurants.

In mid-February, the publisher dispatched Bautzer to negotiate with Folsom. Bautzer quickly learned that Folsom had moved to Las Vegas from Hawaii, where she operated a very successful bordello. The widow did not have a lawyer, nor did she want to hire one, preferring to handle all her own business.[5] After an entire day and night of tough negotiating, Folsom sold Bautzer the property for $84,000.[6]

Under Wilkerson's specific instructions, Bautzer purchased this land in his own name. Wilkerson was known as a high-roller in Las Vegas and his open interest would have inflated the selling price. To increase security, the deed itself was not even recorded until November 21, 1945, some eleven months after the sale.[7]

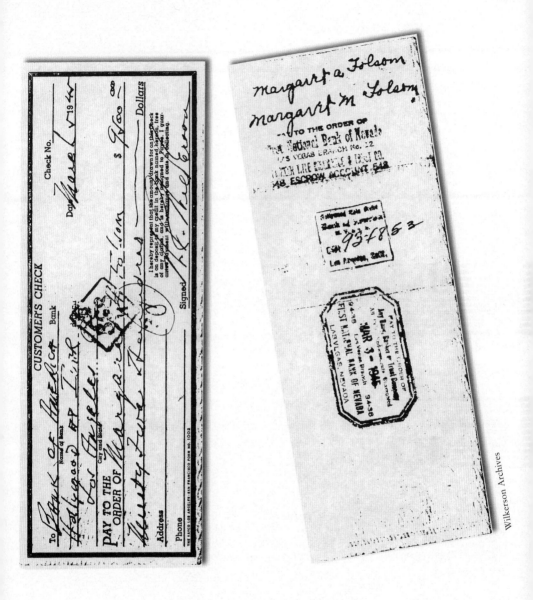

*Partial payment to Margaret Folsom for the Flamingo land.
March 5, 1945.*

What Wilkerson did not know was that his purchase of
Mrs. Folsom's property had inaugurated modern-day Las
Vegas. He was embarking on a momentous undertaking –
one that was far riskier than any financial endeavor. It was
an extraordinary adventure which the publisher would
come to bitterly regret.

5. The Plan

When the Folsom purchase became common knowledge, many felt that Wilkerson had made a mistake by buying land out of town, far from the other hotels and casinos. Friends and colleagues dismissed Wilkerson's Las Vegas venture as a particularly crazy gamble. Unlike him, they couldn't see beyond southern Nevada's hot desert and harsh climate. Wilkerson however, was very pleased with both the land and his idea.

As usual, he had his reasons for buying land so far out of town. First, he needed at least thirty acres and such a large lot was unavailable in Las Vegas itself.[1] Second, he wanted to avoid the competition. He knew most of the casino owners personally and had struck up several good friendships. None of them welcomed competition.[2] Third, the remote location would clearly distinguish his lavish creation from the less imposing gambling operations in town.

George Kennedy remembered that the established operators had cause to feel threatened.[3] Those familiar with his employer's track record knew that he possessed both the means and the talent to duplicate that success locally. If Wilkerson was truly serious, he could cut deeply into their profits. The operators began to worry about the small but steady flow of customers through their doors. They also began pondering the impact of Hollywood's legendary high-rollers on their small community.[4]

As for the project itself, Wilkerson was determined that the resort would house all his passions under one roof. In addition, it had to be something extraordinary and unique, a gambling Mecca that would strike a stunning contrast to the competition in town. It also had to provide a quiet oasis for visitors who did not wish to gamble. For those who just wanted to relax, the complex would be a luxurious home-away-from-home, an insulated world of fine dining, high-quality floor shows and outdoor activities.[5] Wilkerson first committed these ideas to paper in early 1945.

The publisher knew that only the most breathtaking venue would lure patrons into Nevada's searing desert. Once they arrived, something equally stunning would be needed to entice them to remain.[6] In late February 1945, Wilkerson summoned architect George Vernon Russell and decorator Tom Douglas to his Hollywood office. Both men had worked extensively on his Hollywood projects. Society architect Russell had remodeled Wilkerson's Cafe Trocadero in Hollywood in 1936. In 1940 he designed the highly popular and successful Ciro's. Tom Douglas had helped Russell decorate Ciro's. He was also a decorator to the stars whose clients included among others, Greta Garbo, Cary Grant, Carole Lombard, and Clark Gable.

During this initial meeting with Russell and Douglas, Wilkerson outlined his vision for several hours.[7] To fill the 33 acres he envisioned a mammoth complex housing a casino, showroom, nightclub, bar-lounge, restaurant, cafe,

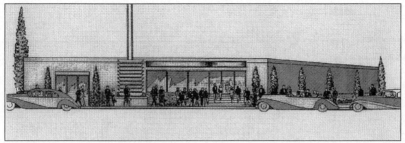

Original rendering of the Flamingo exterior by Bert Worth based on ideas and drawings by George Vernon Russell. November 1945.

hotel, indoor shops, and a health club with steam rooms and a gym. Outdoors there would also be private bungalows, a swimming pool, tennis, badminton, handball and squash courts. A nine-hole golf course would also grace the property. For the more adventurous there would be a trap-shooting range and stables housing forty-five horses.

Wilkerson also wanted to include a sophisticated restaurant along the lines of his Hollywood and Beverly Hills ventures. Four top chefs were to be recruited from Europe. Superb menus, glittering table service and attentive waiters in black tie and tails would be standard. The richly appointed cafe would be Parisian in ambiance.

The publisher also ordered up a luxury hotel for his gamblers. Initially, he had felt that the local accommodations would be adequate. But despite their exotic names, "hotels" like the El Rancho and Last Frontier were little more than rustic motels by today's standards. While they possessed their own unique charm, Wilkerson doubted these establishments could complement the grandeur of his lavish casino, restaurant and nightclub. His vision called for Paris, not the Western frontier. It also called for crowds in numbers that would swamp existing accommodations.

Even if the small town's hotels were able to handle the anticipated volume of visitors, his high-rolling guests would be reluctant to trek several miles in search of overnight accommodation.

Wilkerson decided to build the largest hotel in Las Vegas. It would be five stories tall with two hundred and fifty rooms. Up until 1941, the El Rancho was the largest hotel in Las Vegas with 110 rooms. The Last Frontier followed in 1942 with 107 rooms. His hotel would offer First Class accommodations along European lines. Luxurious and elegant, it would be designed to attract an upscale Beverly Hills clientele. Each hotel room would be decorated with sumptuous appointments and top quality fixtures. Wilkerson instructed Douglas and Russell to pay particularly close attention to the bathrooms. He wanted them modeled on Parisian hotel bathrooms, each with its own sunken bathtub, and something rarely seen in the U.S. – a bidet.

There was also to be a spa and health club facility similar to those at Baden Baden, Germany, where weary gamblers could relax in mineral baths and enjoy massages.

Each of the ten retail stores to be located within the hotel would carry internationally-renowned merchant trademarks. While the idea of stores under hotel roofs was not new, no other establishment in Las Vegas would be able to boast the elegance of Cartier and Chanel from France.

At least thirty private six-room bungalows, modeled on those in the highly successful Beverly Hills Hotel, would surround the hotel's main section. A gigantic showroom similar to the one in Paris's Moulin Rouge would offer floor shows nightly. These entertainments would be modeled on the legendary shows at the Folies Bergères, a favorite of Wilkerson's. There would also be a nightclub similar to his other ventures, offering dancing and sophisticated entertainment after dinner. Top flight live acts and popular bands from his Hollywood venues would be featured.

Then he turned the discussion to the casino. Wilkerson explained to the two men that he wanted to make it as easy as possible for patrons to lose their money. Here his goal was to design an ultra-gambling experience, a complete escape that allowed gamblers to indulge their passion in palatial luxury. It was to be an environment designed to encourage gamblers to lose themselves completely in the thrill of "the action".[8]

In an effort to assist Douglas and Russell, Wilkerson spoke openly to them about his own gaming compulsion. He told them that when he gambled nothing else in the world mattered. At the gaming tables, he lost all track of time. The outside world ceased to exist. He hated to be disturbed or interrupted and confessed that these "lost weekends" were the inspiration for his luxury resort.[9]

He went on to make it clear that he was creating this project to indulge his gambling habit free from the looming fear and worry of bankruptcy. Since he would own the "house", he could gamble in relative safety. The only way the house would lose is if he won and walked away with his winnings.

The overall objective was to feed the gambler's illness, nourishing the compulsion. Isolation, seclusion, and privacy are all key factors in the problem gambler's maniacal quest. Wilkerson was keen to capitalize on the desolate surroundings and Las Vegas' geographical isolation. Clearly, he was well-positioned to provide his designers with detailed insights into the gambler's psyche. He wanted his own debilitating addiction transmuted into the casino's design.

The layout he had in mind was radical. It called for the casino to be placed at the center, "the hub" of the hotel. No guest would be able to move around the hotel without passing through the casino. There would be no windows. "Never let them see daylight," he commanded.[10] Based on his own experience, Wilkerson believed that daylight interfered with the gambler's concentration. No sunsets or sunrises would be visible from the crap or black-jack tables. No wall clocks would be installed, and the lights would be permanently dimmed.

These elements, Wilkerson argued, would mask and conceal the true time of day, ensuring that time passed largely unnoticed. In the gambler's mind, it would always be night.

Wilkerson also wished to make the gambling experience as comfortable as possible. Before 1945, most gaming tables had hard edges.

"They were very much like kitchen tables," remembered George Kennedy, "but covered in felt."[11]

Wilkerson ordered custom gaming tables with curved edges and leather cushioned padding around the sides for extra comfort. He also felt that standing diminished the pleasure of the game. Chairs and stools would be mandatory at every table.

Above all, the casino had to be a gambling palace. He insisted that his creation match the elegance and sophistication of Monte Carlo and Evian. Evening dress would call for black tie.

Wilkerson commissioned Eduardo Jose Samaniego to design the exteriors, from the swimming pool area to the landscaping. In Wilkerson's estimation, there was no finer landscaper. Samaniego submitted drawings and a proposal which included a thirty-foot waterfall and landscaped acres overflowing with exotic plants and flowers. Since there was a complete absence of lush greenery in the desert, whole nurseries were to be transplanted from Los Angeles.

The publisher took into account that all this would require an enormous supply of fresh running water. Building such a project in Las Vegas before 1933 would have been impossible. Fortunately, Boulder Dam had been constructed in the early 1930s, ensuring the town a seemingly limitless fresh water supply.

This gambling vision would be embellished by one final luxury. In addition to the harsh and unsightly topography and the remoteness of the location, there was one last challenge – the weather. The excruciating desert heat seldom varied except during the winter months. Most hotels relied on natural ventilation and electric overhead ceiling fans to cool their rooms. A few hotels even employed swamp coolers – crude devices that were generally ineffective.

"They were noisy, wet, and damp," said Herb McDonald, recalling his days as the assistant general manager of the El Rancho Vegas in 1945.[12]

Wilkerson's project would be the first hotel in the U.S. to utilize the latest innovation in indoor cooling – air conditioning. With it, the desert would at long last become genuinely habitable.

There was also the question of a suitable name and logo for his new enterprise. Wilkerson usually named his projects long before they were completed. The inspiration for most of these exotic names came from his many travels. He was especially fond of conjuring up the glamor of Paris or Rome – Vendome, Cafe Trocadero, LaRue, Ciro's. He also had a particular liking for exotic birds and even named some of his projects after them, like his restaurant L'Aiglon in Beverly Hills. It was no coincidence that one of his favorite nightspots was The Stork Club in New York City.[13]

After considering several ideas, all variations on exotic birds, he finally settled on the name of a magnificent pink bird he had seen during a trip to Florida. Upon completion, the Flamingo Club would take the name of this wondrous creature and come to symbolize all the beauty, grace and elegance of its counterpart.[14] As a final touch, pink flamingos would strut majestically across an artificial lake on the Flamingo's grounds.

Finally, Wilkerson commissioned Hollywood graphic artist Bert Worth to design the logo for his new Las Vegas operation.

The venture was Wilkerson's most adventurous project by far. He envisioned another Sunset Strip in the desert. Although the advent of a hotel-casino-restaurant-showroom in Las Vegas was hardly original, the Flamingo's massive ambition, the grandeur and spectacle of its sprawling size and tone was distinctly impressive. Before the Flamingo, for instance, no Las Vegas hotel had a golf course or such an array of outdoor activity on vast landscaped grounds. There was also the scope of its chic elegance. Prior to Wilkerson, no one had ever thought, much less attempted, to bring glamor to the desert on such an opulent, dramatic scale.

As usual, the publisher's vision was elitist. He was essentially unconcerned with the casual gambler. His new project would cater only to the wealthy and powerful and become a playground for the rich.

"Mr. Wilkerson was adamant that if his patrons were going to gamble, they would do it in style," recalled George Kennedy.[15]

Before Douglas and Russell went to work, Wilkerson reiterated to the two men that everything was to be designed with his own enjoyment in mind. The design had to be so mesmerizing and luxurious that gamblers would be reluctant to leave and eager to return. As he had always done before, he gave Douglas and Russell a free hand. But what he was asking them to do seemed impossible – to duplicate what they had successfully accomplished in ritzy Hollywood in dusty Las Vegas. Transporting the glamor and romance of Paris to Hollywood was one thing; hauling it out to the desert was quite another.[16]

6. The Boys

Although he had never built a casino before, Wilkerson knew enough to realize that no gambling operation could succeed without expert assistance. In his quest to create a first-class casino, he turned to skilled and experienced professionals who knew how to hire high-quality employees, from the croupiers to cashiers, lookouts and undercover security guards.

Farming out the gambling operation of a casino to independent contractors was common practice. Casino owners regularly divided up the various tables and games to skilled operators who provided their own unique talents and bank.

"Mr. Wilkerson's steadfast philosophy had always been 'you get what you pay for,'" recalled Wilkerson's general manager George Kennedy. "He believed that if you hired and bought the best, you got the best. It was that simple."[1]

Wilkerson locked in certain people, such as the chefs at his restaurants, to his various projects by bringing them on board as silent partners. The profit participation was usually so lucrative that few ever had serious thoughts about leaving.[2]

Gus Greenbaum and Moe Sedway knew their business

51

well. In 1945, they were running the El Cortez Hotel and had made a particular success of its gaming tables.[3] When Wilkerson solicited their help to realize his gambling dream, Sedway initially expressed skepticism.[4] Wilkerson's vision was too grand and too far out of town to lure local customers and insure any steady profit. But Wilkerson was not building for the locals. He intended to replicate his success in Hollywood and attract a high-society Beverly Hills clientele. They, not the locals, would bring in the big money.

"The Boys," as he affectionately referred to Sedway and Greenbaum, were excited about the project and ready to accept his offer.[5] For a percentage of the gambling profits and a silent partnership, they would manage and operate the casino and assume total responsibility for every facet of the gaming. They also agreed to help procure all necessary gambling permits.

But both men had shadowy pasts. Greenbaum was an Arizona bookmaker with a police record. He was also a wizard at casino management who later shepherded both the failing Flamingo and the Riviera hotels to enormous profits during the early 1950s.

Moe Sedway was the faithful lieutenant of organized crime czar Meyer Lansky. Sedway had his own police record dating as far back as the early 1920s in New York. He began making trips to Nevada on Lansky's behalf in the early 1930s to franchise the syndicate's Trans-America Wire Service.[6]

It was an effective match. Even though he was a gambler, Wilkerson knew little about the operation and management of a gambling establishment. By the same token, Sedway and Greenbaum lacked the publisher's flair for creating glamorous successes.

Designers Russell and Douglas did not disappoint. Indeed, both men, in comparison to what they had accomplished for Wilkerson in Hollywood, outdid themselves. Russell drew up magnificent plans for the mammoth complex, and Douglas created beautifully detailed designs for the interiors and decorations. Glittering chandeliers, fine woods, polished mirrors and costly marbles would be everywhere. The upholstery was to be plush and elegant, gilt and velvet.[7]

But as the plans grew, so did the project's budget. The building and completion estimates now totaled just under $1,200,000. Although Wilkerson accepted this figure, he did not have the ready cash to invest in the Flamingo. As much as he loathed borrowing, he approached the Bank of America for a loan. Normally banks clamor after successful high-profile businessmen like Wilkerson. This time, however, they declined to lend him the full amount. They politely reminded him that they had extended him a line of credit of $200,000 the previous year, which he had used to cover gambling losses.

"They were aware of Mr. Wilkerson's gambling," said George Kennedy. "Naturally, they were wary about risking a large sum they may not get back. That he was an extremely successful businessman didn't matter. A gambler was a gambler to the bank."[8]

Bank of America eventually agreed to finance $600,000 of the publisher's dream if he used his successful businesses as collateral. Surprisingly, additional funding came from longtime friend Howard Hughes, who owned a number of film-related businesses in Hollywood and had an annual advertising account with the Reporter. Wilkerson told Hughes that he needed $200,000 to build a project in Las

Vegas. Hughes thought Wilkerson was crazy to have anything to do with the Nevada desert. But unlike Wilkerson, Hughes was no table or card gambler. Two decades later, however, Hughes was to follow in his friend's footsteps and invest heavily in the desert town.

Under the pretext that it was a year's pre-paid advertising, Hughes advanced Wilkerson the needed funds without question.[9]

But the impresario was still $400,000 short of his dream. With characteristic confidence, he decided to make up the difference at the gaming tables.[10] This was a terrible mistake. He risked $200,000 in April, only to lose it all.[11]

Unable to afford his initial vision, he asked Russell and Douglas to scale down the plans to accommodate a smaller budget. The blueprints and designs were subsequently modified to include only a casino, restaurant and cafe. Optimistic as ever, Wilkerson predicted that the casino, once in full operation, would bring him the necessary funding to complete the rest of the Flamingo.

For months in 1945 Wilkerson talked enthusiastically about his project.[12] Then came a stunning about-face. He suddenly bowed out of the Flamingo. Conceding that his gambling had gotten the better of him, he decided that remaining involved in the project would only aggravate his habit. Fearing for his financial safety, he vowed to have nothing more to do with gambling and never to return to the source of his temptation. Las Vegas was not for him.

In a letter to Moe Sedway, officially turning the Flamingo over to him and Greenbaum, Wilkerson put it this way:

> I have become convinced that Las Vegas is too dan-
> gerous for me. I like gambling too much, like to shoot
> craps and drive myself nuts and the only way I can
> defeat it is to keep away from any place that has it.
> And that is what I'm going to do.[13]

Some of Wilkerson's friends believed he was just using this latest gambling binge as an excuse for bowing out of an already overwhelming operation. But in reality, Las Vegas had genuinely come to represent his nemesis. After losing close to $10,000 in a single afternoon, he was angry. "I was so disgusted with myself", he wrote.[14]

It was the wrong time to be losing cash. Funds dog-eared for the acquisition of badly-needed new printing presses for The Reporter had been gambled away on this trip. Wilkerson needed $60,000 to cover the purchase. The alternative was to finance the equipment, something that he was adamantly opposed to, as he loathed paying inter-est.[15] Like his father, Wilkerson was a cash man.

In addition to this problem, the publisher owed Moe Sedway an additional $5,000. Wilkerson persuaded Sedway to deduct this debt from the $9,000 he had left invested in the property.

Sedway was of course, familiar with Wilkerson's gambling problem. To prevent the project's land being lost as a result of Wilkerson's gambling, the two men had struck an agreement earlier in the year. Fervently believing in the publisher's project, Sedway agreed to cover any debts Wilkerson had in exchange for a bigger slice of casino profits and ownership in the land.[16] During the course of the year, after nibbling away at his construction funds, Wilkerson had, as his gambling debts increased, turned more and more of the property over to Sedway. By

early September, he had gambled away his remaining ownership in the property, and, on September 15, 1945, deeded the land to Sedway.[17]

In his letter to Moe Sedway, Wilkerson even went so far
as to suggest that the original idea of a hotel was a bad one,
and that the costs of building and operating such a venture
would be prohibitive.[18] This indicates the lengths he was
prepared to go to in order to be rid of the project, and distance himself from his habit. However, the letter also
stressed that the resort he had planned would be, "rich,
sufficiently big and could be built economically and when
opened, few if any would try to create something in opposition to you." He assured Sedway and Greenbaum that no
one was in a better position than they were to accomplish
this.[19] In closing he added:

> I want you to know that I will be happy to be of any
> service, that will not take me to Las Vegas. I can be of
> much help to you here in talent, in seeing that you get
> a good crew for your dining room and kitchen and
> other things which I would be delighted to do. It's my
> impression that you will be much better off without
> me.[20]

Interestingly, this letter makes no mention of Ben Siegel,
nor any suggestion that there was a major and command-
ing figure in the syndicate behind Greenbaum and Sedway.
This helps us understand why these two men took control
of the Flamingo immediately after Siegel's death. It also
makes it sound as if the resort had been their project before
Siegel claimed authorship.

Content with their success at the El Cortez, however,
"the Boys" did not proceed with the Flamingo after
Wilkerson's departure, despite the publisher's blessing and
encouraging words.

By nature, Wilkerson was an emotionally impulsive man. Throwing in the towel on the Flamingo was not out of character for a man who often canceled projects purely on a whim. But if he believed that parting company with the Flamingo project would also bolt the door on his addiction, the publisher was sadly mistaken. Within days he was back at the tables in Las Vegas. Throughout 1945, the publisher gambled like a man possessed, dropping as much as $27,500 in a single day at one casino alone.[21]

Fortunately, Joe Schenck had been taken with Wilkerson's Flamingo from the beginning.[22] He saw its rich potential and appealed to his friend to consider resurrecting the project.[23] The movie tycoon argued persuasively. In another abrupt about-face, Wilkerson re-purchased the Folsom land from Moe Sedway on November 21. With renewed vigor, the publisher forged ahead, totally committed to making his Flamingo a reality.[24]

From the moment Wilkerson bought Margaret Folsom's land to the day he broke ground was almost a year. Construction on the Flamingo Club began in late November 1945. The project, for building purposes, was known as W. R. Wilkerson Enterprises.[25] The builder was Bud Raulston, another person Wilkerson had worked with extensively on his Hollywood projects. Raulston began by bulldozing the two dilapidated "motel" shacks. Within six weeks, foundations had been laid for the kitchen, bar and dining room; a basement excavated and the piping completed. Soon, all the main girders for the building's shell had been erected. Nearly a third of the construction, based on the modified blueprints (that excluded a hotel), was complete before Wilkerson ran into unexpected difficulties.[26]

In the immediate post-war period, labor was plentiful but wartime regulations and restrictions still made building materials extremely scarce. When materials could be obtained, they were invariably astronomically expensive. These inflated costs soon exceeded Wilkerson's budget.[27] He had already sunk $300,000 into the operation. His current gambling losses and debts to Moe Sedway brought the grand total to just under $400,000. In a last-ditch attempt to raise an additional $400,000 capital for completion costs, Wilkerson turned once again to Lady Luck. He staked $150,000 of his remaining $200,000 at the gaming tables and lost it all.[27]

With the majority of his construction capital now gone, Wilkerson looked desperately to Hollywood. The studios were constantly building and dismantling movie sets. Wilkerson offered bargain-basement advertising rates in exchange for surplus lumber and metal. He cajoled several studio heads into donating materials from their back lots.[29] The publisher even went so far as to threaten some movie executives that key movies would not be reviewed unless they agreed to provide him with supplies.[30]

But these scavenged supplies added little of real value to the construction effort, and by early January 1946, Wilkerson's project had ground to a complete standstill. Dismayed, he paid everyone off in cash and left the Flamingo's shell lying like the skeleton of some strange giant, beached in the hot, empty desert.[31]

As the publisher reached the end of his financial tether, Moe Sedway was bringing Billy Wilkerson's project to the attention of Meyer Lansky. Sedway saw it as a unique opportunity for their group to expand operations in Las Vegas. He accurately predicted that the post-war demand for "entertainment" would be enormous. According to his calculations hordes of gamblers from every state in the union would soon be flooding into Las Vegas. They could either prepare for this massive influx or lose out to the competition.

At first, visionary Lansky did not share Sedway's rosy opinions about the future of gaming in the Nevada desert. He hated the searing heat which he believed would keep visitors away from Las Vegas. Lansky had pictured Wilkerson's operation as a modest casino and nightclub and doubted whether they alone would be enough to draw the crowds Sedway spoke of to an unspeakably hot desert. But once Sedway reported on the grandness and scale of

Flamingo construction site, Spring 1946.

Nepwork Photos

Wilkerson's schemes, Lansky began to see visions of money being made in the air-conditioned desert. A decision was taken to invest in Wilkerson's project.

The first step was the approach to Wilkerson. Someone unknown to the publisher had to make him an offer he could not refuse. The site stood empty for well over a month as Wilkerson teetered on the brink of abandoning his dream project.[32]

In late February 1946, he and his builder Bud Raulston were touring the construction site when an expensively dressed man drove up and approached them. He introduced himself as G. Harry Rothberg, a businessman from the east coast.[33]

In reality Rothberg was a man with a dubious past. He and his brother Sam had made their fortune trading liquor. During Prohibition they were the largest and most powerful bootleggers and distributors of black-market liquor in the state of Illinois.[34] Post-Prohibition, Sam continued to create the brew at a new plant in Pekin, Illinois under the banner of the American Distilling Company, Inc., and his brother Harry distributed it through Regents Wine and Liquor Distributors of New York which he owned.[35]

Rothberg said he represented a firm in New York that wished to invest in the Flamingo Club. He and his associates knew that Wilkerson was broke and were willing to help him complete his Las Vegas venture.[36]

Rothberg outlined his proposal. In exchange for funding, Wilkerson would retain a one-third share in the project. Included was the contractual promise that he would call all creative shots. When the club became operational (no later than March 1, 1947), Wilkerson would be its sole operator and manager; all others would be silent partners.[37]

Rothberg asked Wilkerson how much capital he needed to complete the project. Without hesitation the publisher replied, "One million dollars." Rothberg said that if the deal went through, Wilkerson would be advanced completion funds totaling that amount, with a guarantee that he "would not have to put another dime of his own money into the project."[38]

Rothberg was charming. He gave his verbal assurance against any outside interference and flattered Wilkerson by telling him he was the only individual who could complete this task. Wilkerson thanked the mysterious gentleman and said he would take the offer under consideration.

Wilkerson hesitated. The deal meant that he would be handing over two-thirds ownership of his project. It was a big price to pay. He also wondered how Rothberg had found out so much about his plans and finances. The publisher had never put out the word that he was looking for a partner or that he was short of funds. Despite a willingness in the past to make silent partners out of certain key associates, such as his chefs, he had an intense aversion to outside financiers. All too often, such partnerships resulted in constant interference and disastrous balance sheets.

While Wilkerson disliked partners, he had no qualms about investors – people who put up cash in exchange for a slice of the profit pie and then got out of the way. Rothberg's deal, which gave him complete creative and managerial control and a substantial cut of the action, seemed to offer these acceptably silent investors.[39]

Overall, Wilkerson found the Rothberg proposal attractive. He agreed to all Rothberg's terms save one. He demanded he retain complete ownership of the land. Rothberg consented.

"Billy, after a considerable amount of soul searching on

it," recalled Bautzer, "agreed to go ahead and accept the deal."[40]

Under Meyer Lansky's direction, Harry Rothberg organized a syndicate of investors to buy sixty-six percent of Wilkerson's Flamingo. This would be the group's first large investment in Las Vegas. With a million dollars at stake, the Flamingo was also by far, their boldest and riskiest venture.[41]

On February 26, 1946, a contract was signed between Rothberg and Wilkerson.[42] In early March, W. R. Wilkerson Enterprises received $1,000,000 to complete the Flamingo Club, which Wilkerson renamed, the Flamingo Hotel.[43]

With a year to meet his deadline, Wilkerson happily resumed construction. But the ink on the contract had not been dry more than a month when Little Moe Sedway and Gus Greenbaum, both of whom the publisher had already done business with on this same project, visited the construction site. They brought with them a loudly-dressed character who enthusiastically presented himself to the publisher as his new partner.

This man was Ben Siegel.[44]

7. The Investors

Wilkerson was no stranger to organized crime. He had rubbed shoulders with criminals since the Prohibition era. During those troubled times, he had run speakeasies for Mayor James "Jimmy" Walker in New York, and he later owned several of them himself.[1]

During his "speak" days in the early 1920s, Wilkerson relied heavily upon gangsters for the booze that kept him in business. Their efficiency left an indelible impression upon him. And, true to his maxim of always employing the best, he never hesitated to hire them as consultants, brokers or operators in his businesses – from booze to gambling.

If we are judged by the company we keep, then it is indeed difficult to separate Wilkerson from organized crime. His list of friends and connections in the underworld was a veritable "Who's Who" of its most notorious figures – from Hollywood union boss Billy Bioff to Las Vegas mega-gangster Moe Dalitz.

Wilkerson, however, was not a gangster. Even though he was self-employed in nefarious activities which brought him under the scrutiny of federal law agencies, he never threatened or killed people for a living. Nor did he get involved with racket activities such

Wilkerson, speakeasy owner. New York, Fall 1924.

as wire services or numbers, or participate in either prostitution or narcotics. But, as the U.S. Board of Tax Appeals aptly put it: "Wilkerson's life has been a successful though precarious one."[2]

Not surprisingly, Wilkerson's love of gambling brought him into regular contact with organized crime. After gambling was outlawed in California in 1938, high rolling gamblers such as Wilkerson often fell prey to organized crime scams in backroom card games.

Wilkerson also mixed with gangsters at his restaurants and clubs where they dined frequently and, more often than not, wanted to meet him. They paid social calls at his office and home. Wilkerson, in turn, brought them lavish gifts from his travels. He also provided special favors such as the best seats in his clubs and invitations to important movie premieres.

Whether Wilkerson cultivated these relationships for genuine friendship or as insurance, they certainly brought him rewards. When general strikes (usually influenced and backed by organized crime) plagued Hollywood in the 1940s, Wilkerson's businesses were miraculously spared.[3] In 1942, when he feared for his personal safety, he paid gambling ship proprietor Tony Cornero $6,500 for his allegedly bulletproof, custom-built, pale blue Cadillac.[4]

"Wilkerson should have been a gangster," commented Edith Gwynn, the publisher's second wife, "but he didn't have the guts."[5]

The relationship between Billy Wilkerson and his new partners was extremely delicate. Most had links with organized crime or were already crime figures. In addition to career criminals, the group consisted mainly of polished businessmen and religious conservative Jews like Meyer

Lansky. In exchange for funding to complete his project, Wilkerson gave these men a vital link with legitimacy. They were well aware of the publisher's credibility and "Midas Touch" reputation as a businessman. His impressive track record had fueled their decision to invest in his project. They were also well aware of the value of using a high-profile legitimate name to front their activities. Wilkerson would be the magnet that would draw high-rollers from Beverly Hills.

Wilkerson could hardly have known at the time he negotiated with Harry Rothberg, that he was making a pact with the devil, or that he was about to give Nevada its largest ever influx of organized crime.

It is not known when Benny Siegel and Billy Wilkerson first met. It has been hinted that the two knew each other as early as the publisher's New York speakeasy days. They were certainly acquainted by 1936 when the gangster dined at Wilkerson's nightspots. It was no secret, for instance, that Siegel had a particular affection for Ciro's, one of Wilkerson's hottest nightclubs. By day, the gangster was also a regular at Wilkerson's Sunset House, the barbershop and haberdashery where he enjoyed close personal ties with the shop's main barber, Harry Drucker. Drucker always made sure that Siegel got the best shave, facial, haircut and manicure of the day.[6] Another point of contact between the two men was Agua Caliente, the gambling facility on the Mexican border where Wilkerson spent a great deal of his leisure time.

In 1942, Siegel's notoriety became impossible to ignore when he went on trial for the November 1939 murder of Harry Greenberg.[7] The high-profile case attracted widespread public attention in the Los Angeles. When matinee idol George Raft testified for his Hell's Kitchen friend, crowds

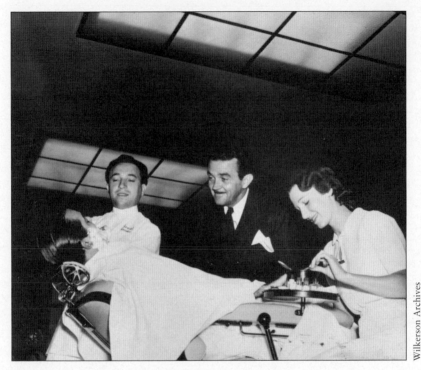

Billy Wilkerson looks on as client "sportsman" Ben Siegel gets a shave from Harry Drucker. Hollywood, 1936.

flocked to the courtroom. Siegel's preferential treatment in jail was a hot topic at Hollywood's society parties. He refused to eat prison food and had Wilkerson arrange for Ciro's finest meals to be delivered to his cell. He was allowed female visitors and was even granted leave for "dental visits".

Shortly after the trial began, the two main witnesses against Siegel and his accomplice, Frankie Carbo, suddenly died. The district attorney was then stripped of his case, and he dismissed all charges against Siegel and Carbo on February 5 due to insufficient evidence.[8]

Hollywood and the gangster were made for each other.

Siegel loved the Sunset Strip, the night-life, the clubs. But he was especially smitten with the film industry. He mingled with the stars, was invited to celebrity parties and sat at the best tables in all the top restaurants and nightclubs.

Although Benny quickly established himself as a social butterfly and a playboy on a par with Howard Hughes, he was regarded as a failure in town.[9] Little of what he did during his sojourn was noteworthy. At one stage, "sportsman" Siegel briefly flirted with the idea of becoming a movie star like boyhood friend and matinee idol George Raft. The naive but ambitious Siegel financed his own 8x10 glossies and even paid for a screen test.[10] But his ego prevented him from starting at the bottom of anything and so seeking work as an extra or a common actor was out of the question. He was, after all, Ben Siegel. Ironically, Siegel had only to ask the influential Wilkerson for help. His pride, however, prevented him from doing so, and the gangster's film career never got off the ground.

Siegel's personal income during this period remained a great source of mystery. While never proven, it was said to be enormous. There was an estimated take from racetracks, races and race wire services in the neighborhood of $20,000 a month. It was rumored that he owned a small percentage of Agua Caliente, the Tijuana facility frequented by Wilkerson and other Hollywood notables. Siegel apparently also owned a piece of The Clover Club in Hollywood close to Wilkerson's successful Cafe Trocadero. This club thrived on legal gambling until the 1938 crackdown. From time to time the gangster was even known to play the stock market (without success). Yet while Siegel was known to call gamblers "suckers," his gambling addiction rivaled Wilkerson's.

Even though the studio gates stayed firmly closed, Hollywood opened its bedrooms to the gangster. He enjoyed the celebrity status of a movie star. At that time the town was fascinated with gangsters, and Siegel could not have found a more perfect setting for his incessant womanizing. The likes of Betty Grable, Lana Turner and Ava Gardner, as well as millionairess Countess Dorothy Difrasso and many others, were seen on his arm. Ben found himself mired in romantic, and very public, complications, and soon his notorious love life attracted the attention of his gangster colleagues. They advocated anonymity in professional life and stability in domestic life. Siegel, who, they were quick to note, was both a Jew and a married man, was urged to keep a lower profile.

Siegel's romantic troubles peaked in 1945. The man who could have practically any woman he desired laid claim to a plump aspiring actress from Alabama. Few could see what attracted the suave Siegel to the vulgar Virginia Hill. She was certainly no beauty. According to Virginia, her lock on Siegel was based on an ability to arouse and satisfy his sexual needs.[11] But in truth Siegel recognized himself in Hill – headstrong, stubborn and street-wise.

There were two distinct and opposing sides to Benjamin Siegel's nature. Many were familiar with his warm, easy-going charm. In this role, Ben was typically attentive and vibrant; at times, even boyishly innocent and reserved.[12] But his grace and dashing looks disguised a dangerous bully. This dark side typically revealed itself in sudden violent outbursts that some likened to epileptic seizures. These fierce rages, which would suddenly take hold of Siegel, were frightening to behold. To make matters worse, the merest incident could ignite his temper and provoke him to acts of homicidal violence.[13]

"His face would darken when he got angry," Greg Bautzer remembered, "and his blue eyes were known to turn a slate gray color."[14]

Friend Harry Drucker recalled Siegel this way: "It was rare that Ben got angry. But when he did, he really let go."[15]

"Mr. Siegel was not the sort of man you got angry," remembered George Kennedy. "Even worse, he never forgot why you got him angry. It gave new meaning to the word 'grudge.'"[16]

Unfortunately for Ben Siegel, this unflattering trademark which branded him in life, became his enduring legacy in death. Moreover, Siegel's public temper tantrums became a source of acute embarrassment to publicity-shy crime syndicate members.[17]

Siegel was not a Mafia prince like Meyer Lansky or Johnny Rosselli. Although his power and influence have never been disputed, he was certainly not in their league. Siegel was viewed more as a loose cannon than a clever entrepreneur like his friend Meyer; nor did he possess Lansky's brains and uncanny business acumen. Although he dressed flamboyantly, like a movie star, Siegel worked hard to cultivate the image of the cutthroat gangster. While other gangsters acquired curious nick-names that echoed their various traits and idiosyncrasies, Benjamin Siegel distinguished himself by his ruthless ability to make good on threats uttered in anger.[18]

"Anyone who knew Siegel took his threats seriously – or was wise enough to," said Greg Bautzer.[19]

Siegel often employed violence as a means of getting his

way. He viewed murder in particular as a convenient solution to problems which would not go away on their own. In the spring of 1946, unhappy about the performance of one of his crew, Wilkerson called a late-night meeting with Siegel, architect George Vernon Russell, and decorator Tom Douglas.[20] They stood around a table reviewing the blueprints in an unfinished room of the Flamingo dedicated as a "plan room". It was next to a small room Siegel had converted into a makeshift gym where he lifted weights.

A furious Wilkerson vented his frustration. "This guy's driving me nuts. I wish to God someone would take care of him!"

In a voice from a different world Siegel said, "I'll take care of him, Billy."

The room fell silent. There was no mistaking what the gangster meant.

Panicked, Wilkerson responded quickly. "Shit, no. Not like that!"[21]

Although the mobster seemed to embody good manners and charm on the surface, he suffered from a complete lack of modesty. On one occasion Siegel summoned his architect Richard Stadelman to his penthouse suite at the unfinished Flamingo to discuss business. The gangster was bedridden but not with illness. He simply chose to conduct business from his bed. What was even more unusual was that while Siegel casually rambled on and on, Stadelman noticed, with acute embarrassment, that Siegel was completely naked under the single sheet, with an equally nude Virginia Hill by his side. Not once did it dawn on Stadelman's employer that there was anything abnormal about this situation.[22]

Much has been written about Siegel's tough gangster image, but little is known about the sentimentality he infrequently displayed. On one rare occasion, George Kennedy, Wilkerson's general manager, was privy to this tender side.[23]

Siegel was meeting with Wilkerson in his publishing office one Saturday morning. At around 11:30, George Kennedy, who was taking notes, received a call that his elder brother Harry was dying. Kennedy asked to be excused and returned three hours later, crestfallen.

Siegel immediately noticed Kennedy's change in demeanor. "What happened, George?" he asked.

"There was genuine concern in Mr. Siegel's voice," Kennedy remembered.[24]

"My brother died in my arms, Mr. Siegel," replied a grief-stricken Kennedy.

Kennedy requested the rest of the day off, but, in typical Ebenezer Scrooge fashion, Wilkerson refused. The taskmaster reminded his employee that there was simply too much work to be done around the office.

Siegel followed Kennedy out into the corridor as he walked back to his office. From his pocket he produced the thickest roll of $100 bills Kennedy had ever seen. Tear-stricken, Siegel pressed the entire roll into Kennedy's palm. "Take it, George. Go on, take it."

Touched by this display of sympathy and generosity, Kennedy thanked the gangster but politely refused his offer.[25]

8. The Hotel

Like many of his gangster counterparts, Siegel yearned to be legitimate. When he first came to Hollywood, he set out to shed his gangster image and reinvent himself. He detested his nick-name in particular because it was an ugly reminder of a thuggish past. Nobody dared call Ben Siegel, "Bugsy" to his face. Yet, while he basked in Hollywood's glamor and embraced its lifestyle, his love affair with the movie capital brought him only notoriety. The perfume of the legitimacy and respectability he craved was still well beyond his reach. But by the spring of 1946, that perfume became stronger – wafting in on the heat waves of Wilkerson's Flamingo. Las Vegas gave Benny Siegel his second opportunity to re-invent himself.

Like Wilkerson, Benny Siegel hated the desert. It was the only thing he hated as much as his ugly nick-name. He had originally traveled west to southern Nevada in the 1930s with Meyer Lansky's lieutenant Moe Sedway, on Lansky's orders to explore the possibilities for expanding their operations. From the moment he first set foot in the Nevada Desert, his compelling hatred of it became apparent. Like his friend Meyer, Ben Siegel could not understand what anyone would want with the place. Life in the

73

windswept desert was certainly not to the young gangster's liking. Lansky had turned the desert over to Ben Siegel. But Siegel, wanting nothing to do with it, turned it over to Moe Sedway and fled with lightning speed for the lights and glamor of Hollywood – lured, like so many others, by delusions of stardom. Vowing to avoid the desert at all costs, he made his home in Beverly Hills.

Sedway, on the other hand, remained behind in Las Vegas to establish a race wire service. Soon, he was running the El Cortez Hotel with Arizona bookmaker Gus Greenbaum for a syndicate of investors which included, among others, Siegel and Lansky.[1]

Lansky pressured Siegel to represent them in Wilkerson's desert project. Someone had to watchdog their interests. Siegel, who knew Wilkerson and lived near him in Beverly Hills, was the obvious choice as a liaison. But Siegel was infuriated. He wanted no part of any operation that took him back to Nevada on a permanent basis. It meant forsaking his comfortable Beverly Hills nest and Hollywood playboy lifestyle and enduring the sweltering heat of the Nevada Desert. At Lansky's insistence, however, Siegel reluctantly consented.

Wilkerson was shocked to discover that his new partner was Ben Siegel.

"You can imagine how he felt," said Kennedy.[2]

"It was Billy's decision to concern himself with the eventual outcome and success of his project," said Bautzer, "rather than on connections his business associates might have had."[3]

The track records of the two men could not have been more different. Siegel was a notorious gangster whose dubious activities included bookmaking, running wire services and killing people. Unlike his friend and underworld cohort Meyer Lansky, Siegel had never built anything. Wilkerson, in contrast, was a suave, debonair entrepeneur who created showcases of splendor which were also commercial successes. He wielded enormous influence and power in the film industry.

In Hollywood, the charming, well-mannered gangster deferred to Wilkerson on everything.[4] In fact, Siegel went overboard to win Wilkerson's approval. He charmed his way into the publisher's office, showering his staff with lavish gifts in an effort to gain easy access to their employer.

As George Kennedy vividly remembered: "Wanting to see Mr. Wilkerson, he always came to the office with gifts. Mr. Wilkerson got a lot of clothing. I got mostly silk neckties. He was always extremely cordial in his dealings with Mr. Wilkerson. A real gentleman. He could charm the wrappings off a mummy. And whenever Mr. Wilkerson needed something done, Mr. Siegel saw to it immediately."[5]

Throughout the spring of 1946, Wilkerson and Siegel met almost daily at the publisher's office. He worked closely with Wilkerson, assisting him in every way possible. Wilkerson gave Siegel tasks to perform and welcomed suggestions from the gangster.[6] Siegel soon proved remarkably useful to Wilkerson. He obtained black-market building materials through his connections. The post-war shortages that had dogged construction were no longer a problem.

One afternoon in late March 1946, Siegel and Wilkerson were standing at the construction site.

"One day," commented Wilkerson, "there will be hotels lined up and down this road as far as the eye can see."

"Why?" an astonished Siegel asked. "Why would anyone want to come here?"

Wilkerson looked at Siegel. "Because of people like me. People will endure almost anything, go anywhere where there is legal gambling."[7]

As the two men worked together, it became increasingly obvious that the young arrogant gangster idolized his partner and aspired to imitate him.[8]

"Siegel did not want to be like Billy," remembered Tom Seward. "He literally wanted to be Billy."[9]

Since the early 1940s Siegel had been in awe of the impresario.[10] Wilkerson's restaurants, lifestyle and reputation appealed to the gangster who'd been raised in the grimy slums of New York. Siegel reasoned that if anyone could be his passport to legitimacy, it was Wilkerson.[11] The venture also gave him a great excuse to leave his Hollywood disappointments behind and head out into the desert.

At first Siegel seemed content to do things Wilkerson's way. His desire to learn everything about the project from the ground up took precedence over his "sportsman" lifestyle. It also seems to have temporarily subdued his aggressive impulses. Under Wilkerson's tutelage, Siegel played the willing pupil, earnestly learning the mechanics of building an enterprise.

"Siegel did not know a bidet from a Bordeaux, much less marbles from Italy," said Tom Seward. "Billy showed him everything."[12]

Wilkerson shipped Siegel off to his professionals – architects, builders and decorators, who, at his request, patiently schooled the thug from Hell's Kitchen.[13] Colin Russell, the architect's son, remembers that, "Siegel would sit in my father's office for hours soaking up all the information."[14]

Unfortunately, the role of pupil did not come easily to Benny Siegel. Perhaps outdistanced and afraid of being upstaged by his mentor, Siegel began to feel intimidated and paranoid.[15] He grew increasingly resentful of Wilkerson's talents and vision. As time went on, the gangster's respectful admiration disintegrated into an insane, all-consuming jealousy.

That Siegel should have suffered from such extreme envy is hardly surprising. He was a highly competitive man who rarely allowed himself to be outdone by anything or anyone. Once the teacher-student relationship wore thin, Siegel's long-festering jealousy began to infect his relationship with the publisher.[16]

"Siegel was so jealous of Billy it drove him crazy," remembered Tom Seward.[17]

It all started quietly enough. Siegel reverted to his familiar role; the big-shot. He began making decisions on his own without Wilkerson's consultation or authorization. Informing work crews that Wilkerson had put him in charge, Siegel ordered changes which conflicted with the blue-printed plans.[18]

"Mr. Wilkerson would give an order, then Ben Siegel would reverse it," recalled George Kennedy.[19]

Wilkerson was understandably furious. When he confronted the gangster, Siegel sheepishly apologized, only to resume his autocratic behavior once Wilkerson's back was turned.[20]

Then, taking credit for Wilkerson's vision, Siegel began boasting that the Flamingo had been his idea.[21] Soon, the mere mention of Wilkerson's name would send him into a spasm of red-faced, fist-pounding rage. Asked what Wilkerson's participation was, Siegel would angrily refer to his partner as something tantamount to a mere workman.[22] On at least one occasion he shouted at a questioning reporter, "This is my fucking hotel! My idea! Wilkerson has nothing to do with it! Do you understand? Nothing to do with it!"[23]

At first, it seemed that Siegel was perfectly content to remain in Beverly Hills where he made his home. But as the project grew and took shape, so did his ambitions. It was simply impossible for a man like Siegel to remain on the sidelines. He had to be running the show. He saw himself at the helm of a luxurious establishment. He would be Las Vegas's self-appointed gambling czar.[24]

The problem came to a head when Siegel openly protested his watchdog role. He demanded more hands-on involvement in the project from his mentor.[25] Wilkerson refused. But Siegel's behind-the-scenes interference started slowing the project's pace. In an effort to appease the gangster and keep the project moving smoothly, Wilkerson agreed to a compromise.[26] George Kennedy recalls that the project was partitioned.[27] It was mutually agreed that Siegel would supervise the hotel portion while Wilkerson retained control of everything else.[28]

Siegel asked Wilkerson to find him an architect and a contractor. He readily obliged the gangster, hiring architect Richard Stadelman and Phoenix contractor Del E. Webb.[29]

The construction project was split into two distinct halves. Siegel had his crew and Wilkerson had his. There was little or no communication between the two sections, and soon the operation fell into a welter of disarray and mayhem. Neither man would have anything to do with the other.[30]

Siegel's jealousy manifested itself even further when he went into furious competition with Wilkerson. He became drunk with power. Within a month he had spent the funding allocated for the hotel portion and stridently demanded more from Wilkerson's budget. Wilkerson refused.[31]

"Siegel was out of control," recalled Bautzer. "Where Billy was sticking to his budget, he was not."[32]

Wilkerson had every reason to be worried. Siegel's unchecked extravagance was alarming.

"Mr. Wilkerson knew he was dealing with a lunatic at that point," Kennedy remembered.[33]

Wilkerson's only hope was that the powers behind Siegel would awake to the situation and fire him. He reasoned that he could still make the venture a success so long as Siegel was stopped in time.

Unfortunately, the publisher's wish was not to be granted.

9. The Nevada Project

As time passed, Siegel's grandiose ambitions mushroomed into uncontrolled greed. Unhappy with the business arrangements originally negotiated by Harry Rothberg, the gangster began to view Wilkerson, who held the reins of power, as a major obstacle. In May 1946, Siegel decided that the original agreement had been a mistake. It had to be altered to give him full control of the Flamingo.

Meyer Lansky, who had left his mark on so many previous projects, was strangely absent from the venture. In an uncharacteristic move, he stepped aside and turned Las Vegas over to his friend Benny.

Siegel began by gaining the wary syndicate's support. Using the momentum he had generated by badgering Wilkerson out of the hotel portion, Siegel persuaded his skeptical partners to let him take the helm. The gangster gave them strict assurances that under his charge there would be no changes – Wilkerson would not be eliminated from the creative process.

Wilkerson, however, quickly realized that Siegel, far

from mending fences, was instead bent on destroying him. For his part, Wilkerson no longer relished his business or personal relationship with Siegel. He found the gangster's irrational behavior abrasive and his unpredictable rages unsettling.

Siegel offered to buy out the publisher's creative participation, not with cash, but corporate stock – an additional 5 percent ownership in the operation. Although Wilkerson did not welcome the idea of relinquishing complete control, Siegel's many flaws made his decision easier. He accepted the offer. Without seeing the hook, he swallowed the bait.

On June 20, 1946, Benny formed the Nevada Project Corporation of California, naming himself as president. He was also the largest principal stockholder in the operation, which defined everyone else, including Wilkerson, merely as shareholders.[1] Although the publisher remained a sizable shareholder, and still owned all the land, the Nevada Project Corporation heralded the end of Wilkerson's creative participation and the beginning of Siegel's absolute autonomy. From this point on the Flamingo became effectively a syndicate-run operation.

The brief friendship between the two men was also now at an end. After the incorporation, Siegel could not get rid of Wilkerson fast enough. With Wilkerson now a mere stockholder, the Flamingo was Siegel's, interference free. He never consulted Wilkerson again and wasted no time in implementing his own plans.

W. R. Wilkerson Enterprises underwent an astounding change. Siegel fired all Wilkerson's on-site associates and staff. Decorator Tom Douglas and architect George Vernon Russell were replaced by Del Webb and Richard

Stadelman.[2] Responsibility for the interior decorations was delegated to Siegel's girlfriend, Virginia Hill.[3]

Wilkerson had been stripped of all creative control and relegated to a mere shareholder. His duties as hotel manager could not begin until the hotel was finished. Seeing no point in remaining in Las Vegas, he returned to Hollywood.

To Wilkerson and those close to Siegel it was clear that the gangster knew little about building a large resort. By late July it became evident to everyone except the man in charge that he possessed neither his partner's expertise nor the vision to pull off something of this magnitude.

"He had no idea what he was doing," declared George Kennedy.[4]

The original Flamingo budget became an ever more distant memory as Siegel grew increasingly dictatorial and autocratic. He became an instant expert on everything, refusing all advice and insisting on making every decision himself.

Prior to seizing creative control from Wilkerson, Siegel used the publisher's reputation to raise more cash for the project from the consortium. At first, this ploy worked well because no one within the syndicate's ranks contacted Wilkerson about Benny's additional financial requests.

Siegel then began spending with a free hand. Ignoring Wilkerson's meticulous plans, Siegel launched an all-out spending spree that was staggering even by today's standards. He indulged his taste for the astronomically expensive by demanding the finest building that money could buy at a time when wartime shortages were still being felt.

"Siegel just didn't want marble," remembered George Kennedy. "He wanted the finest, most costly Italian marble there was."[5]

Soon, the site swarmed with construction equipment and materials all supplied through Siegel's connections.[6] Carpenters, plasterers and other workmen were flown in and paid handsomely, sometimes as much as $50 a day.[7]

Siegel decreed that each bathroom of the ninety-three room hotel should have its own private plumbing and sewer system. Cost: $1,150,000.[8] More toilets were ordered than needed.[9] Cost: $50,000. Because of the new plumbing alterations, the boiler room, now too small at its original capacity, had to be enlarged. Cost: $113,000.[10] Siegel also ordered a larger kitchen. Cost: $29,000.[11]

The main Oregon Building featured 77 luxurious rooms, with 16 fire exits. Siegel's extravagances included the construction of a lavish fourth-floor penthouse in the main building of the hotel for his private use. For security reasons, Siegel ordered up an escape hatch in the closet of his suite. This led to an intricate labyrinth of secret passageways and staircases which were also used for smuggling women and gangsters into his room. Although many of the Oregon's staircases led nowhere, if you knew the layout, it was possible to descend to the garage and a waiting getaway car in less than a minute.

The steel ceiling beam crossing Siegel's living room was too low for the gangster, who kept hitting his head on it as he paced the carpet. He ordered it moved. Cost: $21,750.[12]

The Flamingo's catastrophic cost over-runs have always been blamed on Siegel. But his newly appointed interior decorator, the strident Virginia Hill, also helped inflate the ballooning budget. Virginia, a failed actress, was totally unqualified for this crucial role. Often, Benny left her in charge of the entire operation while he was away on fund-raising trips desperately hustling for cash. Virginia's decisions regarding the construction and building would invariably be countermanded by Siegel on his return. After Hill ordered heavy, expensive curtains for the main lounge, Benny took one look at them and knew that they were highly flammable. Even the foolhardy Siegel understood the importance of fire precautions. The nearest fire station was seven miles away. The drapes had to be removed and returned to Los Angeles, where they were chemically treated for fire proofing.[13] Nonetheless, Siegel continued sheepishly acquiescing to Virginia's demands for drastic, costly changes. Some felt this obedience was an attempt to curry favor with his domineering girlfriend.[14]

But by far the most stupefying cost was Siegel's frenetic building, destruction and rebuilding. Amazing amounts of concrete were poured into the building. Siegel, departing radically from Wilkerson's vision, ordered architect Stadelman to build an enormous plate glass window in the casino so that gamblers could have a view of the pool. This idea presented itself only after Wilkerson had built a solid wall there to exclude all natural light.

During remodeling in the mid-1960s, it took a wrecking crew working with a giant iron ball three days to demolish a single wall of the hotel. In the old casino, dislodging and removing a banister taxed a battery of jackhammer operators for two days.[15]

Adding to the budgetary over-runs were problems with dishonest contractors and disgruntled unpaid builders. By day, trucks regularly delivered black market goods. By night the same materials were often pilfered, and resold to Siegel a few days later.[16]

As costs soared, Siegel's checks began bouncing. One sizable check to Del Webb was returned to the contractor stamped "Insufficient Funds."[17] Humiliated, Siegel abjectly apologized, assuring the contractor that the funds would soon be in hand.[18] But an irate Webb took his revenge. Angered by Siegel's non-payment, he ordered trucks full of materials, checked them onto the Flamingo site, charged them to the corporation, and then dispatched them to a different building project at another location. Nothing was unloaded at the Flamingo.[19]

"If he couldn't get his money, he was going to take it out in materials," said Kennedy.[20]

Siegel's dream of owning the Flamingo outright was still unrealized. As yet, one crucial element remained – the land. Contractually, this acreage belonged to Wilkerson under the terms of the February 28 agreement. Siegel schemed to obtain full possession of it from the publisher. Benny offered Wilkerson a percentage of corporate stock in exchange for his land. Wilkerson agreed to sell half his property for an additional 5 percent stake in the Nevada Project. Siegel accepted, and on June 26, 1946, Wilkerson and Siegel signed an agreement to this effect.[21]

"Mr. Wilkerson believed he would make far more money owning a bigger share of corporate stock than asking for a cash buy-out for the actual land," remarked George Kennedy.[22]

But Siegel was still unhappy. He brooded over the remaining half, and in early August, approached the publisher to sell his final parcel of land. Again the gangster offered corporate stock. And again Wilkerson agreed, but insisted on another 5 percent as payment. Siegel accepted. On August 22, 1946, an agreement reflecting this exchange was executed between the two men.[23]

This brought Wilkerson's shareholding total in the corporation to 48%, making the publisher the largest single shareholder in the Flamingo.

By October 1946, the project's costs had soared above $4 million. In the spring of 1947, the Flamingo would clock in at over $6,000,000. Ben's senseless extravagances were becoming all too apparent. As finances skyrocketed out of control, the same partnership that had so eagerly lent its support to Siegel's take-over now openly questioned his effectiveness. Few of them possessed Meyer Lansky's vision, imagination and innovative flair. Despite their dubious and illegal professions these were, in the main, very conservative men when it came to lifestyle and cash. They disliked taking risks with their money, and they actively sought out business opportunities that were already proven commodities. They were more concerned with making a modest profit than spending lavishly on something as grandiose and unproven as the Flamingo. The record shows that prior to 1946, they mostly bought into existing operations in Nevada, like the El Cortez, that were already showing a safe and steady return. The majority of these investments were, at best, only modestly profitable. Now they were losing millions.

Wilkerson was of course fully aware that speculation was growing regarding the Flamingo's true budget. He was still close enough to the project to sense the enormous cost overruns. But a secretive Siegel remained tight-lipped about the project's accounting. Wilkerson and those representing him could only speculate about the true amount being spent.[24]

"Mr. Wilkerson tried cautioning Mr. Siegel about his spending," recalled George Kennedy. "But his advice fell on deaf ears."[25]

Despite the unpleasantness, the publisher took consolation in the fact that his deal with Siegel promised to make him a very wealthy man. On one memorable occasion in his Hollywood office, the publisher even said as much to the gangster's face.[26]

"For every buck you put into this deal," Wilkerson reminded Siegel, "forty-eight cents is mine."[27]

"Mr. Wilkerson laughed at him," recalls George Kennedy. "Mr. Siegel didn't like that. That wasn't the way you talked to Ben Siegel."[28]

The first indication of trouble for the gangster came in early November. The syndicate issued a stern ultimatum: either provide them with a full accounting or forfeit future funding. But the last thing Siegel wanted to do was produce a balance sheet. Instead he countered by pressuring Wilkerson to sign a bank loan for a substantial amount to keep the project afloat. Wilkerson was understandably furious. He reminded Siegel that he had both a signed agreement and Rothberg's verbal assurance that he would not have to invest any additional money.

Siegel replied, "This is still your deal, too. If you don't sign, we all go under."[29]

Even for a seasoned gambler, it was a difficult call. If Wilkerson refused to sign, Siegel might be unable to continue, the project would collapse into bankruptcy and Wilkerson would lose his entire investment. He would probably also be blamed for bringing the Flamingo crashing to the ground. Signing for the loan, on the other hand, meant pinning his hopes to the remote possibility of future success.

The thought had also crossed Wilkerson's mind that Siegel might be bluffing by saying that he needed cash when he really didn't. It could all be just a ploy on the gangster's part to suck him deeper into the project.

"Billy was put in a very difficult spot," remembered Greg Bautzer.[30]

In the end, supporting the gangster seemed the only rational choice. Against his better judgment, on November 29, 1946, Wilkerson signed a loan with the Valley National Bank of Phoenix, Arizona, for $600,000. Wilkerson was the sole signatory. Sadly, it was only a drop in the ocean.

After the syndicate's refusal of help, Siegel waged a reckless campaign of private fundraising. He was so desperate for cash that he even sold nonexistent stock. Some, like Wilkerson's lawyer, Greg Bautzer, believed that Siegel would have signed anything for money at this point. Making matters worse was Siegel's self-imposed secrecy. His reluctance to disclose details about the project only fueled the syndicate's doubts. With his unchecked extravagance no longer in dispute, the question of what to do about this loose cannon began to overshadow all other considerations.

Suddenly, Siegel was in a hurry to finish the hotel. Much against Wilkerson's advice, he doubled his work force, believing the project could be completed in half the time. But it was the costs, not the building, that began rising even faster. Siegel paid overtime and even double-time. In some cases, special bonuses tied to project deadlines were offered in hope of increasing productivity.[31]

By the end of November work on the casino was nearly finished. Under immense pressure to have the hotel start making some money, Benny moved up the grand opening from Wilkerson's original date of March 1, 1947 to the day after Christmas, 1946. Although the hotel portion was still incomplete he was hoping to generate enough revenue from the casino to complete the project and repay angry investors. Siegel formally announced that the hotel would be open and ready for occupancy the day after Christmas. Its gala opening would be held that same evening, December 26, 1946.

Back in Hollywood, Wilkerson, who had known from its inception that the Flamingo was at the very least a four-teen-month project, took Siegel's decision badly.

"The hotel was not finished. The casino was barely ready," George Kennedy remembered. "Mr. Wilkerson was fit to be tied. He paced the floor, yelling at the walls, 'That mother-fucker, what the fuck does he think he knows?'"[32]

In a phone call to the gangster in Las Vegas, Wilkerson vehemently rejected the December opening date.

"They really locked horns over the date," recalled Kennedy.[33]

Wilkerson argued that opening on December 26 was tantamount to commercial suicide. The hotel would not be ready in time. The casino would lose money if there were no hotel rooms available for the guests to stay in while they gambled. Even worse, opening during the holidays made no sense whatsoever.[34] People in the entertainment industry were accustomed to staying home during the final two weeks of the year.

The gangster ignored Wilkerson's solemn warnings. Siegel was desperate for fast profits which would pull him out of his financial nosedive. Wilkerson pointed out that, in the real business world, such expectations were totally unrealistic. If it happened, it was by accident. To Ben Siegel, impatience was a way of life. He was counting on such an accident or what Wilkerson later called "a major

Catholic miracle."[35] Hot-headed and agitated, Siegel shouted into the phone: "I'm the one who makes the decisions!"[36]

Unable to communicate with the erratic gangster, Wilkerson hung up, stoically surrendering to the prospect of total failure.

10. The Meeting

One morning, Vic Enyart, Wilkerson's star advertising sales executive, happened to be in the publisher's office when the head of the FBI called.[1]

"Billy, I remember, didn't say anything. He just listened, which was unusual for him. As he listened, I watched his face turn white as a sheet. He said, 'Thank you' and hung up. 'That was Hoover,' he said to me, 'He's warning me about Siegel.'" [2]

It is not certain when or how the relationship between Wilkerson and J. Edgar Hoover began. It seems likely that they first met during one of Hoover's many visits to the West Coast.[3] No correspondence or photos of the two men together survive, but, according to several third party accounts, they enjoyed a cordial if formal relationship.[4] Their shared interests included a love of race tracks and a mutual hatred of "reds." The FBI director was especially supportive of the anti-Communist campaign Wilkerson waged in Hollywood during the late 1940s and early 1950s. Time and time again, Hoover supplied the publisher with vital information in his war against Hollywood's "red subversives."

In later years, particularly after the war, the G-man continued this helpful habit, alerting the publisher to potentially dangerous business contacts.[5]

"Hoover had called Wilkerson to warn him of the possibility of a complete syndicate takeover of the Flamingo and that his life might be in danger," said Greg Bautzer.[6]

But Hoover's warning about Siegel, which arrived in early December 1946, came too late. Wilkerson was already deeply involved. Any attempt to extricate himself would have jeopardized his entire investment.[7]

Wilkerson decided to make the best of a bad situation. He would bolster his investment by making sure the outside world knew about the Flamingo. He hired press agent Paul Price in Los Angeles. Together the two men began formulating a massive public relations campaign for the hotel's gala opening. Their publicity materials included glossy prints of half-naked, well-endowed young women. Their seductive smiles suggested that there would be plenty of action for high-rollers after they left the tables.[8] Publicity and advertising were Wilkerson's strengths, and he knew his target audience.

He was in the middle of this campaign when Siegel called a stockbrokers' meeting at the unfinished hotel. The meeting took place in mid-December, two weeks before the Flamingo's opening. Present were lawyers representing Siegel, Louis Wiener and Clifford A. Jones. Jones at the time was Lieutenant Governor of the State of Nevada.[9] Moe Sedway and Gus Greenbaum who had originally been Wilkerson's partners in the Flamingo's casino accompanied Siegel to the meeting.[10] Wilkerson attended with his legal counsel, Greg Bautzer.

"Billy's interest made him the largest individual stockholder in the venture," Bautzer recalled. "He owned 48 percent of $6 million. He was dealing from a position of immense strength."[11]

Siegel got straight down to business.

Siegel (to Wilkerson): "You're gonna have to part with your portion of the interest."

Wilkerson (to Siegel): "What am I going to be paid for it?"

Siegel (menacingly): "You're not going to be paid anything for it, and you'd better have all the interest in hand."

Wilkerson began to speak, but his attorney interrupted. Meeting Siegel's force with equal force, Bautzer responded in kind, taking care to use language the gangster would understand.

"Just a minute," he said to Siegel. "Are you telling this man, who has a legal and valid right to the interest, that he's gonna have to part with it? 'Cause he's not gonna have to do anything."

Siegel shot back. "He's gonna have to do this because I've sold 150 percent of this deal, and I don't have 150 percent. It's only 100 percent and everybody's gonna have to cut including Billy."

To which Bautzer replied, "Well, you'd better figure another way out, 'cause he ain't gonna cut."

Siegel jumped to his feet, shaking with anger, yelling at Bautzer: "I can only tell you if I don't deliver the interest to the people in the East, I'm gonna be killed." Turning to Wilkerson he continued, "And before I go, you're gonna go first. And don't take that lightly. I'll kill ya if I don't get that interest."

Bautzer stood up and yelled back at Siegel. "Sit down and shut up!"

He then ordered his client out of the room and laid down a stern warning to the gangster and his attorneys: "I'll tell ya what I'm gonna do. You'd better shut this guy up 'cause I'm gonna make an affidavit on the remarks Mr. Siegel has made at this meeting and who was present. I'm sending one copy to the District Attorney of Los Angeles. I'm sending one copy to the District Attorney of the county here in Las Vegas. I'm sending one copy to the Attorney General. And I'm sending one copy to the FBI. And if Mr. Siegel is wise, or his associates here are, they'd better make sure Mr. Wilkerson doesn't accidentally fall down a flight of stairs. They'd better make sure he doesn't sprain an ankle walking off a curb, because that affidavit is going to be in the hands of those men, and I'm going to be prepared to testify like all the rest of you are going to have to testify as to the statements Mr. Siegel has made. So they'd better be goddamn sure Mr. Wilkerson enjoys a very long and happy life."

Siegel's attorneys chorused: "Nothing is going to happen to him, so take it easy, Greg. There's no need for affidavits, or going to District Attorneys."

Bautzer shouted back, "I don't care! That's what I'm gonna do and he'd better be made aware by you gentlemen that represent him of the consequences of that if anything does happen to Billy."

And with that, Bautzer stormed out.

Wilkerson learned from the aborted conference that the stock he had been sold by Siegel was either worthless or did not, in fact, exist.

"Mr. Wilkerson received 'toilet paper' for his interest," George Kennedy commented.[14]

Strapped for cash, the gangster had secretly oversold the project. As a result, Siegel was facing a cash-flow problem of gargantuan proportions. Benny's dream of owning the Flamingo outright was evaporating in front of him. He evidently hoped that if he owned Wilkerson's percentage he could use it to leverage enough cash to complete the enterprise and bail himself out with his irate partners.

News of Siegel's overselling stunned both Wilkerson and Bautzer. It made the publisher question the value of his share. What was clear was that Siegel had no intention of honoring legal obligations, especially those he had signed with Wilkerson.

The second thing the publisher learned from the ill-fated meeting was that killing meant little to Ben Siegel. Until that meeting he had usually managed to ignore both Siegel's unsavory occupation and his hair-trigger temper. The gangster's personality defect now came home to haunt him, adding a horrifying new dimension to the debacle. In voicing his loud threats, Siegel had made it abundantly clear that Wilkerson's fate was inextricably linked to his own. In short, the publisher's failure to comply would result in both their deaths.

Wilkerson and Bautzer returned to the El Rancho Vegas where they were staying. On the drive back, Bautzer asked Wilkerson where he had gone after he had left the room.

Wilkerson's reply was blunt, "To the john."

"For the first time, Billy realized his life was in danger," recalled Bautzer.[15]

Back at the hotel Wilkerson reviewed options with his attorney. They could give the dangerous gangster exactly what he wanted. While Wilkerson would most likely walk away with his life, his entire investment would be forfeited. The only alternative was to stand firm against Siegel's outrageous demands.

Bautzer felt sure that the gangster's death threat had been made in earnest. He recommended that his client leave Las Vegas immediately. Even in the hotel room his safety could not be guaranteed. He told Wilkerson to leave matters to him. He would handle the negotiations in his absence.

While Bautzer made out the affidavits, Wilkerson ordered some food and made his travel arrangements to fly back to Los Angeles. When room service arrived, the publisher had lost his appetite.

"He was unusually quiet," recalled Bautzer of his client.

An hour later Wilkerson said good-bye to his attorney and a few hours later was back in his Bel-Air home. En route to the plane, Wilkerson made a brief stop at the Nevada State Police Department in Las Vegas. He applied for a permit to carry a concealed firearm.

Around midnight, Bautzer received a phone call from Cliff Jones, one of Siegel's legal advisers. Jones suggested a meeting the following morning.[17]

Bautzer snarled, "Who's going to be present, because I'm not meeting with Mr. Siegel. I've had all the conversation from him I want to have or ever intend to have. I suggest you and myself."

Siegel's attorney insisted on Wilkerson's presence.

"No way," said Bautzer. "You want a meeting, it's going to be without Mr. Wilkerson."

Ben Siegel's counsel reluctantly acquiesced.

When the two men met the following morning, Jones confirmed that Siegel had oversold the project.

Bautzer remembered Jones telling him: "He oversold to try and get enough money flowing to complete this project. He's in a terrible spot. The boys have given him an ultimatum."

"That's his problem," Bautzer replied unsympathetically.

Jones asked Bautzer to tell him Wilkerson's sell-out price. Bautzer said he did not know but would ask his client.

What neither man knew was that Wilkerson had already decided to go into hiding.

11. Paris

The dream project had become Wilkerson's worst nightmare. Instead of waiting for Siegel to act on his gruesome threat, he decided instead to avoid the gangster. All future communications between himself and Siegel were conducted through their respective attorneys and emissaries.

Wilkerson took further steps to secure his safety by catching the first flight to New York, where he boarded an ocean liner, the Ile de France, bound for France. From the French port of Le Havre he made his way by car to Paris, where he booked into the plush Hotel George V under a pseudonym.[1] His whereabouts were kept secret from all but a few.[2]

He phoned his attorney, Greg Bautzer, as soon as he reached Paris, and Bautzer relayed the details of the meeting with Cliff Jones. Wilkerson was not pleased.

"He was reticent about selling," Bautzer remembered. "He said, 'Forty-eight percent of this deal is rightfully mine. Why the hell should I sell?'"[3]

Wilkerson's plan was simple: he would wait in Paris until things cooled down. He predicted, as he had for months, that once Siegel's partners learned about his lavish spending and excesses, it would only be a matter of time before they fired the incompetent gangster. There would then be a change of management under which Wilkerson would retain his interest and would once again be re-instated as creative director. He would then complete his hotel without interference.[4]

In an attempt to accelerate this process, Wilkerson ran ads in The Hollywood Reporter publicizing the hotel's true cost. These lavish full-page ads boasted that the Flamingo had cost more than $5 million. If the syndicate had not already known how much the Flamingo had cost them, they certainly knew now.[5] It was a dangerous ploy.

Wilkerson spent a chilly Christmas in Paris. When the Flamingo opened in Las Vegas, he sat alone in his hotel room eating a quiet dinner and reading the newspapers.[6]

A few days later he learned by phone that his dire predictions regarding the opening had in fact, been overly optimistic. To begin with, Siegel had managed to generate considerable confusion regarding the opening date itself. Acting on a whim, the gangster had suddenly decided that a weekend would be more likely to entice the much-needed celebrities away from home. Invitations were subsequently sent out for Saturday, December 28. Then the indecisive gangster changed his mind yet again. Invitees were hurriedly notified by phone that the opening had been changed back to its original date, the 26.

While locals jammed the opening, the masses of celebrities Siegel had been counting on never materialized. After Wilkerson's departure Ben had tried rallying stars on his own, but few Hollywood celebrities would deal directly with the erratic gangster.

To transport the anticipated star-studded guest roster

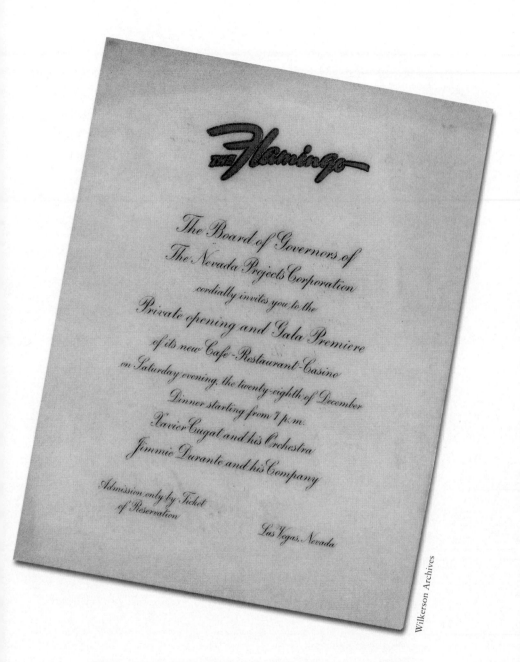

Original invitation to December 1946 Flamingo opening.

from Hollywood to the opening, the publisher had chartered two TWA Constellations from his friend Howard Hughes.[7] If enough celebrities had changed their minds at the last minute, these planes could have been filled. In the end it didn't matter – bad weather plagued Los Angeles on the evening of the 26, grounding all flights.

A handful of celebrities did motor in from Los Angeles despite the appalling weather. Some of the celebrities present were June Haver, Vivian Blaine, George Raft, Sonny Tufts, Brian Donlevy and Charles Coburn. They were welcomed by a cacophony of construction noise and a lobby draped with decorators' drop cloths. The desert's first air-conditioning system collapsed at regular intervals, leaving

View of Flamingo grounds with Oregon Building in the background, not long after its first opening on December 26, 1946.

guests cursing the heat.[9] While visitors did find gambling tables in operation at the Flamingo, the luxury rooms that would have served as the lure for them to stay and gamble longer were not ready. Guests were housed at hotels in town.

Luckily, Wilkerson had arranged the opening night's entertainment months earlier. On stage, things went smoothly. The opening show consisted of Jimmy Durante, George Jessel as master of ceremonies, Xavier Cugat and his band, Rosemarie, Tommy Wonder and The Tunetoppers. All were top stars in their day.

Off stage, it was an entirely different situation. Desperately short of time, Siegel had decided to rely on the kitchen staff, chefs, waiters and bartenders Wilkerson had recruited in Los Angeles. Unfortunately, these new recruits had yet to complete their training. They were thrown into an unfamiliar, unfinished building, prompting numerous complaints about poor service.[10]

Wilkerson's idea of formal attire for the opening was abandoned at the last minute. As a result, the gala event was awash with curious locals who stared in amazement at croupiers and dealers in white tie and tails. Nevada residents sporting cowboy hats were insulted when they were asked to remove them.[11] Wilkerson had always insisted on an all-male staff in the dining room. Siegel retained Wilkerson's idea without realizing that most of the locals were used to being waited on by friendly, chatty waitresses, not formal waiters and aloof captains.[12]

A few days before this fiasco, Siegel's underlings had finally summoned up the courage to tell their boss that all the matchbooks cited Wilkerson as manager. In Las Vegas, "managers" were also the proprietors and owners.

Matchbook of Flamingo showing W. R. Wilkerson as Manager.
November 1946.

Thousands of these books had been printed. In a rage, Siegel ordered everything with Wilkerson's name on it destroyed. Because there wasn't enough time to reprint the matchbooks, some brave soul suggested a number be saved for the opening. Siegel hired a squad of women with black grease pencils to strike out the publisher's name wherever it appeared.[13]

The gangster had also been overly optimistic about the revenues the Flamingo would bring in on opening night. As Wilkerson had predicted, a major reason why the casino lost money when it opened was because there were no hotel rooms available to keep guests gambling after hours. Gamblers and guests alike took their winnings elsewhere. After two weeks of operation the Flamingo's plush gaming tables were $275,000 in the red. Siegel couldn't understand what was happening. In desperation, he speculated that the local desert folk were more cunning than his newly-trained dealers.

His financial windfall having failed to materialize, Siegel shut the entire operation down in late January 1946. By now he blamed everything on Wilkerson.

In Paris, Wilkerson's strategy managed to create the illusion that he was still at his Hollywood desk. He maintained daily contact with the office by phone and telex, and he continued to write his daily editorial column, which he dictated over the phone.[14] In support of this subterfuge, the publisher shunned all the customary pursuits of a wealthy American in Paris. He rarely went outdoors, and even while inside the hotel he kept to himself. If someone recognized him in the lobby he said he was visiting briefly on business. If he was invited to dinner or for a drink, he politely declined the invitation by saying he was leaving early the following morning. His only daily indulgence was to walk to a nearby sidewalk cafe for a Coke and an English-language newspaper. Every Sunday, he made a single major excursion. He took a cab to Mass at Notre Dame Cathedral.[15]

Back in Las Vegas, Siegel's troubles were compounding. The costs of The Flamingo continued to skyrocket. Siegel had spent an additional $750,000 on operating and building costs. By April, the total amount of red ink had soared to an unprecedented $6,000,000.[16] This situation was not helped by Wilkerson who complicated matters by stubbornly refusing to relinquish his interest. Before delivering any accounting, Siegel had been relying on this interest to bolster his figures and offset his extravagant expenditures.

In a series of phone calls to Paris, Greg Bautzer pressed his client to sell the Flamingo. In his opinion, the operation under Siegel was far too unstable to generate any worthwhile revenues.

Wilkerson did not share his attorney's perspective. First, nobody was going to scare him out of a business deal; no one ever had and no one was going to do so now. Second, he was sitting on a windfall. He owned close to half of what would eventually turn out to be a six-million-dollar-plus investment. He anxiously awaited Siegel's firing and the change of management.

But the weeks in exile began taking their toll. The publisher did not feel safe. His sleep was fitful. Since he was confined mostly to his hotel, he felt his life was not his own. He began questioning whether any business deal was worth such deprivations.

In mid-February 1947, Wilkerson reluctantly came to the conclusion that the Flamingo was never going to be his. Until then he had assumed that nobody would take a psychotic gangster seriously. But as the weeks dragged on, he realized he was wrong.

Wilkerson set his sell-out price at $2,000,000. He also insisted on a signed document legally exonerating him from all financial responsibilities in the venture and releasing him completely from any further obligations to the corporation.[17] Bautzer conveyed this offer to Siegel's attorneys. While they agreed to the document releasing Wilkerson from the Flamingo, they balked at the price. They offered $300,000. Wilkerson scoffed. This amount would in no way adequately compensate him for what he was losing.

Concerned for Wilkerson's safety, Bautzer asked his client to consider dropping the amount to $1,000,000. After much cajoling he was successful. When Bautzer relayed the new amount, Siegel's camp countered with a final "take it and get out" offer of $600,000. Wilkerson, reasoning that the dollar amount was insignificant compared to the value of his life, accepted this deal.[18]

Since both Bautzer and Wilkerson refused to meet with the gangster in person, the task of extracting payment from Siegel fell to Wilkerson's business partner, Tom Seward. Seward was dispatched to Las Vegas in late February by Wilkerson and Bautzer on what turned out to be an exercise in futility.

Siegel was in the process of re-opening the hotel. The opening was scheduled for March 1, Wilkerson's original date. He was so determined to get it right this time, he had arranged a dress rehearsal. At the rehearsal, Seward sat next to Siegel in a booth that also held Meyer Lansky. Siegel was clearly annoyed by Seward's presence. Seward was a blatant reminder of the publisher. The fact that he was there to collect money Siegel rightfully felt belonged to him only infuriated the gangster further.

Siegel turned to Seward, made a symbolic revolver out of his hand and pointed the barrel at Seward's head. Seward recalled feeling the pressure of the gangster's fingers against his skull.

"If your partner were here right now I'd blow his fucking brains out," Siegel said.

"It was terrifying," remembered Seward.[19]

Just at that moment, the gangster was interrupted by a phone call. Once Siegel was out of sight, Seward made his excuses and hurried back to Hollywood. Empty-handed, he told Bautzer in no uncertain terms he wanted nothing further to do with the gangster.[20]

The second Flamingo opening was not without its problems. Again the publisher's magic touch was lacking. Although furniture was now installed in most of the rooms, a myriad of problems with the kitchen, plumbing and service drove guests to competing establishments.

Finally, on March 19, both Benjamin Siegel and G. Harry Rothberg signed a formal Release of All Demands releasing Wilkerson from the Nevada Project Corporation.[21] This document effectively absolved the publisher from any wrongdoing in the project. He was to receive partial payment of $300,000 for his interest in early May, with the remaining half three months later in August.

A week later Wilkerson returned to Hollywood. Tony Cornero's pale-blue bullet-proof Cadillac became his transportation of choice. The publisher had not been back more than a few days when his general manager put an urgent phone call through to him.

George Kennedy recalled: "Mr. Wilkerson asked me who it was. I said the frantic woman would not say, but I remember strongly suggesting he take the call."[22]

<u>RELEASE OF ALL DEMANDS</u>

KNOW ALL MEN BY THESE PRESENTS, That BEN SIEGEL and
G. HARRY ROTHBERG, jointly and severally, for a good and
valuable consideration, receipt whereof is hereby acknowledged, do by these presents, release and discharge W. R.
WILKERSON, his agents, employees and representatives, of
and from all demands, and all manner of actions and
causes of actions, suits, debts, dues, sums of money,
accounts, reckonings, bonds, bills, specialties, covenants,
controversies, agreements, promises, variances, trespasses,
damages, judgments, executions, claims and demands whatsoever, in law or in equity, including but not limited to
the following: Any or all claims or obligations arising
under those certain agreements heretofore executed between
the undersigned and said W. R. Wilkerson under dates of
February 26, 1946, June 26, 1946, and August 22, 1946, and
any and all amendments and modifications thereof, which
the said Ben Siegel and G. Harry Rothberg, jointly and
severally, ever had or now has, or which they or their
heirs, executors or administrators, hereafter can, shall,
or may have against the said W. R. WILKERSON, for, upon,
or by reason of any matter, cause or thing whatsoever,
from the beginning of the world to the date of these
presents.

IN WITNESS WHEREOF, we have hereunto set our hands
this _19ᵗʰ_ day of March, 1947.

Ben Siegel

G. Harry Rothberg

*The Nevada Project document signed by Siegel and Rothberg releas-
ing Wilkerson from the Flamingo. March 19, 1947.*

108

Kennedy instructed the switchboard operator to route the call through to Wilkerson's direct private line.[23]

The anonymous caller hysterically begged Wilkerson to leave town immediately. Her husband, newly paroled, "a good man" she said, had been contracted to kill him. She said she didn't want him "mixed up in any more trouble." She reiterated her plea and then abruptly hung up.[24]

Wilkerson must have found the call convincing because within forty-eight hours he was heading back to Paris.

"There was every chance, of course, that it was a bluff," said Greg Bautzer. "I asked Billy not to take the risk."[25]

Bautzer reported the phone call to the police. Radio personality and reporter Walter Winchell got hold of this story and broadcast the news that Billy Wilkerson's life had been threatened. According to Tom Seward, Siegel was called in and questioned by the authorities. Predictably, he denied making any threats against the publisher.[26]

In late April, Wilkerson received confirmation from his attorney that his interest had been transferred to the Nevada Project Corporation. He took two weeks off and spent the time doing the things he found most pleasurable in Paris. Wilkerson saw the sights, went shopping and visited the Moulin Rouge. At night he strolled the city's streets, enjoying the outdoor music. Wilkerson was even comfortable enough to reveal his whereabouts; he now made it no secret he was corresponding from France – his daily Tradeviews were by-lined from the capital.[27]

In Las Vegas, Siegel appealed to his partners for more time to make the hotel profitable. But, having already invested considerable sums, the syndicate members were impatient to see a return. In May, however, he surprised them. The Flamingo was at last making a profit. But it was too little, too late. The gangster's failure to show any significant gains confirmed doubts about his ability to manage the enterprise.[28] In mid-May an impatient syndicate angrily tabulated Siegel's errors. The image of the man they had trusted to mastermind their most important project had radically altered.

By late May, Wilkerson was thinking of returning home for good when his general manager called him with a mysterious warning.[29] George Kennedy relayed the contents of an anonymous phone call he had received advising him to tell his employer to remain in Paris until "it was over."[30] Without identifying himself, the caller had hung up abruptly after delivering the message.

"The caller identified me by name," recalled Kennedy, suggesting that the man knew both him and his employer.[31]

In light of the call in early April that had driven him back into hiding, Wilkerson had an uneasy feeling about this message. He decided to act on the warning and delayed his departure from Paris. Fearing transatlantic reprisals, Bautzer cautioned his client to remain in his hotel room as much as possible.

Nearly two months later, on the morning of Saturday, June 21, Wilkerson bought his newspaper, sat down at a sidewalk cafe and ordered a Coke. When he unfolded the paper, he saw the article and immediately returned to his hotel.

Waiting for him was a cable from his general manager in Hollywood. Kennedy's cable confirmed the newspaper story. On the evening of June 20, as he sat reading a newspaper in longtime girlfriend Virginia Hill's rented Beverly Hills house, an assassin had riddled Benjamin "Bugsy"

Siegel's body with bullets from a .30-30 military carbine. Hill was conveniently away in Paris at the time.[32]

Minutes after the shooting, Moe Sedway and Gus Greenbaum took possession of the Flamingo. No one questioned or disputed their authority.

Wilkerson packed his bags and returned to Los Angeles on June 23, 1947. When Kennedy met him at the airport, Wilkerson greeted his general manger in characteristic fashion.

"What the fuck did you waste company money on a cable for? It made every fucking paper!"[33]

Ben Siegel's untimely end, June 20, 1947.

12. The End

I t is not known exactly who orchestrated Siegel's murder. Why he was killed also remains a mystery. There are three main theories. The first is that it was the work of an individual linked to Siegel's bookmaking activities in California. The second is that Las Vegas hotel and casino owners, terrified of a state-wide eastern syndicate take-over through the Flamingo, killed Siegel to head off infiltration into their territory. Wilkerson allegedly participated in, or at least had prior knowledge of this plot to eliminate Siegel. The third, and most widely accepted theory, is that Siegel's own partners killed him.[1]

Certainly Siegel had committed a number of glaring errors in his partners' eyes. He had been secretive and non-disclosing. In the wake of the hotel's highly-unprofitable opening, the syndicate of investors decided that they could no longer overlook Benny's excessive spending. The syndicate ordered him to produce a detailed accounting of the hotel's spiraling construction costs. When this accounting was not forthcoming, they launched an immediate investigation into these expenditures.

While Siegel had insisted that everything was under control, this investigation revealed exactly the opposite. Crooked contractors and unpaid builders had been allowed to swindle the operation. When the syndicate had refused him any more funding until he delivered an accounting, Benny had distributed shares to outside investors, and oversold the project by as much as 400%, in order to generate more construction cash.[2] Virginia Hill's incompetence had also contributed to the flood of red ink. There was no evidence of embezzlement, but the syndicate was outraged to learn that the Flamingo Wilkerson had initially promised to deliver for $1 million had cost close to six times that amount. There never was a final accounting while Siegel was alive. The unenviable job of reconciling the figures fell to his successors.

Benny's damaged credibility with his partners may well have prevented him from redeeming himself on any level. It had long been known by his partners that he had no business skills and was terrible with cash. The flashy spendthrift who moved to Hollywood, was also, like Wilkerson, a terrible gambler. Blinded by ego, devoured by his own megalomania, the great business talent Siegel boasted of was not evident anywhere in the Flamingo.

"This was not his business," Bautzer observed. "Prior to the Flamingo, Siegel exhibited no experience in building anything. He was in way over his head."

Bautzer concluded: "Siegel was not the right choice to head an operation like the Flamingo. He was a paranoid man who had no business masterminding a multi-million dollar deal. I blame the principals associated with Siegel, who let him get away with it, as much as I do Siegel. The Flamingo wound up being the most expensive hotel ever built in the world at the time."[3]

In the end, young Siegel was unsuccessful at making the transition out of his gangster world. He suffered, it seems, from an identity crisis of enormous proportions. He never ceased to struggle between two diametrically opposed

worlds. Seigel had fled his gangster past only to be repeat-
edly excluded from the legitimacy and glamor he craved.
And on the evening of June 20, one of these worlds claimed
his life.

A police inquiry into Siegel's death was held on June
25. Detectives visited Wilkerson's Hollywood office and
questioned him about the extent of his involvement in the
Flamingo and the Nevada Project Corporation.[4] The detectives intimated that Wilkerson knew more than he was
telling them. They implied a direct link between the publisher and organized crime based on associations stemming
from his involvement in the project.[5] Wilkerson emphati-
cally denied any connections with organized crime or any
other criminal activity.

But for Billy Wilkerson, the Flamingo chapter was not
yet closed. Although he chose to forget his Las Vegas dream,
the publisher received a rude public reminder in 1950.

In January of that year, Wilkerson drove up to Sun
Valley, Idaho for a week with his bride-to-be Beatrice Ruby
"Tichi" Noble.[6] One evening, during dinner, Virginia Hill
entered the dining room and spotted Wilkerson. She hurried over to his table and exploded with an anger reminis-
cent of Benny's rages.

"It's all your fault, you lousy prick!" she screamed at
the publisher. "It was because of you they killed him!"

People stopped eating and conversations fell silent as
Virginia wildly accused Wilkerson of causing Ben's death.
She claimed that her boyfriend's inability to procure the
publisher's stock had accelerated his untimely demise. Still
yelling, she added that if Wilkerson had only turned over
his interest on time "none of this would have happened."

After ranting and raving at the top of her lungs and

working herself up into a frenzy for what seemed minutes by Wilkerson's reckoning, she slapped his face violently back and forth several times and stormed out of the restaurant.

"The entire room went quiet," remembered Tichi Wilkerson. "After she left you could have heard a pin drop."[7]

Billy Wilkerson never saw Virginia Hill again. For him, this was the last physical remnant of the Flamingo debacle.

What Wilkerson begun and Siegel's successors completed were two separate visions. The new management under Sedway and Greenbaum favored something less intimidating. For example, they departed from Wilkerson's elegant vision by dropping the formal dress code.

"People running around in the middle of a hot desert in black tie and formal attire. It was preposterous," remembered one of Wilkerson's detractors.[8]

Under the new partnership, the Flamingo became a non-exclusive facility – an egalitarian establishment where gamblers could relax and flirt elegantly with Lady Luck at prices affordable to almost anyone.[9] They also made the enterprise extremely successful. In the first year alone, Sedway and Greenbaum turned a $4 million profit.

Wilkerson could not have forecast what Las Vegas was to become. In later years he was awed by the flowering of his idea. The publisher's dream of transforming a sleepy desert community into a luxurious gambling Mecca was far surpassed. The stretch of land several miles out of town where he had first broken ground became crowded with fabulous hotels, each more outlandish than its predecessor; all glittering monuments to his passion for gambling. When visiting Las Vegas, however, he never stayed at the hotel he created.

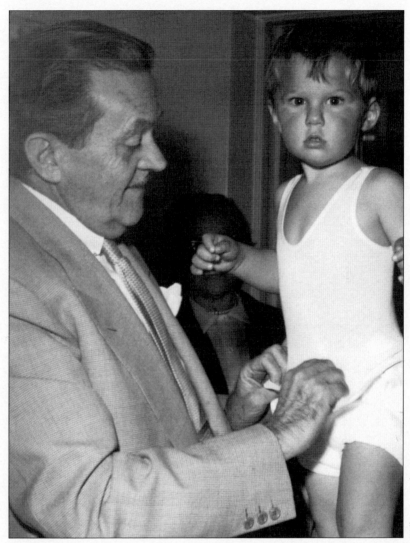

Billy Wilkerson and Willie Jr. Bel-Air, 1953

In the end, it was fatherhood that gave Wilkerson the inspiration to kick the habit which had plagued him for so much of his life. He quit gambling cold turkey with the birth of his son in October, 1951. It was as if family life provided a sense of permanence and fulfillment that had been sadly lacking throughout six nomadic decades. This newfound contentment gave Wilkerson the strength to stop gambling.

He never returned to either the tables or the track again.

Los Angeles
November 1991 – June 1995

Notes

1. THE MAN

1. George H. Kennedy, Jr., interview, August 1972.
2. TIME, July 3, 1944, p. 78.
3. Ibid.
4. TIME, July 3, 1944, p. 76.
5. Joe Pasternak, interview, September 1972.
6. TIME, July 3, 1944, p. 78.
7. Vivian du Bois, interview, October 1972.
8. George H. Kennedy, Jr., interview, August 1972.

2. THE GAMBLING BUG

1. TIME, July 3, 1944, p.76.
2. George H. Kennedy, Jr., interview, August 1972.
3-4. Ibid.
5. Raoul Walsh, interview, September 1972.
6. Howard Kotch, interview, February 9, 1993.
7. Thomas F. Seward, interview, December 15, 1992.
8. Raoul Walsh, interview, September 1972.
9. Thomas F. Seward, interview, September 1972.
10. Ibid.
11-15. George H. Kennedy, Jr., interview, August 1972.
16. A gambling IOU was commonly known as a "marker" or "marker slip". Officially they were known as "cash advance slips".

17. George H. Kennedy, Jr., interview, August 1972.
18. Ibid.
19. Tichi Kassel, interview, August 21, 1991.
20. George H. Kennedy, Jr., interview, August 1972.

3. THE IDEA

1-4. George H. Kennedy, Jr., interview, August 1974.
5. Joseph Schenck, chairman of Twentieth Century Fox Pictures, provided Wilkerson with projection equipment and personnel so that he could view movies in the comfort and privacy of his own home. Howard Strickling, head of the MGM publicity department also provided the publisher with MGM's latest releases.
6. George H. Kennedy, Jr., interview, August 1972.
7. Thomas Seward, interview, December 15, 1992.
8. George H. Kennedy, Jr., interview, August 1972.
9. Ibid.
10. David Alexander, interview, September 1972.
11. George H. Kennedy, Jr., interview, August 1972.
12. Ibid.
13. Letter from Billy Wilkerson to Moe Sedway, undated.
14. George H. Kennedy, Jr., interview, August 1972.
15. Finch & Rosenkrantz, Gone Hollywood, p. 118.
16. Donald O'Connor, interview, May 17, 1994. The entertainer, who performed on the S.S. Rex, remembered that the facilities on these gambling ships were as luxurious as any that existed on land.
17. Finch & Rosenkrantz, Gone Hollywood p. 117. Southern California had its own race tracks by 1935.
18. George H. Kennedy, Jr., interview, August 1972.
19. Estelle Brown Stewart, interview, May 6, 1993. Thomas Seward, interview, December 15, 1992.
20. L. A. EXAMINER Morgue, Regional History Department, October 8, 1941.
21. George H. Kennedy, Jr., interview, August 1972.
22. These men were Milton "Farmer" Page, Eddie Nealis, Al

Wertheimer and Nola Hahn.
23. Thomas Seward, interview, December, 15, 1992.
24. Ibid.
25. Jennings, We Only Kill Each Other, p. 135.

4. THE VISION

1. George H. Kennedy, Jr., interview, August 1972.
2. Tichi Kassel, interview, August 21, 1991.
3. Drown owned the El Rancho Vegas from 1943-46.
4. Thomas F. Seward, interview, December 15, 1992.
5. Greg Bautzer, interview, May 5, 1972.
6. Thomas F. Seward, interview, December 15, 1992. According to Seward there were two separate parcels of property. One was ten acres which Wilkerson originally bought from Folsom. The second was twenty-three acres which he purchased from Folsom at a later date. The land became known as The Folsom Property.
7. Book 40 of Deeds, p. 381-2, Clark County, Nevada. Title first recorded under Moe Sedway then under Greg Bautzer acting for Billy Wilkerson. Both deeds recorded the same day.

5. THE PLAN

1. George H. Kennedy, Jr., interview, August 1972.
2-4. Ibid.
5. Greg Bautzer, interview, May 5, 1972.
6. Thomas F. Seward, interview, September 1972.
7. George H. Kennedy, Jr., interview, August 1972.
8-11. Ibid.
12. Herb McDonald, interview, February 10, 1993.
13. George H. Kennedy, Jr., interview, August 1972.
14-16. Ibid. The Russell and Douglas meeting as related to author by George Kennedy.

6. THE BOYS

1-2. George H. Kennedy, Jr., interview, August 1972.

3. Lacey, Little Man, p. 152.

4. Thomas F. Seward, interview, December 15, 1992. Wilkerson approached the two men in February 1945.

5. Ibid. It is not known what percentage Greenbaum and Sedway received for their participation in running the gaming.

6. Beatrice Sedway, interview, May 23, 1992.

7-11. George H. Kennedy, Jr., interview, August 1972.

12. Thomas F. Seward, interview, December 15, 1992.

13. Letter from Billy Wilkerson to Moe Sedway, mailed to the El Cortez Hotel, Las Vegas, Nevada. The letter is undated.

14. Ibid. Checks: Cash, July 13, 1945, $3,275. Cash, July 13, 1945, $1,000. Hotel Last Frontier, July 14, 1945, $5,000.

15. Thomas F. Seward, interview, December 15, 1992.

16-17. Ibid. The title and deed of transfer of land in Book of Deeds p. 381, Clark County, Las Vegas, reads that the land was formally transferred from Margaret Folsom to Moe Sedway. However, a check from Wilkerson to Folsom dated March 5, 1945 for $9,500 indicates funds were transferred between them eight months before Sedway quitclaimed the property to Wilkerson's attorney, Greg Bautzer. Thomas Seward, then partner to Wilkerson, confirmed that this was, in fact, an initial down-payment to Folsom for the land's purchase.

18. Letter from Billy Wilkerson to Moe Sedway, undated.

19-20. Ibid.

21. Wilkerson's Las Vegas "customer's" checks of this period. March 17, 1945 – The Monte Carlo Club.

22. CLOSE-UP, September 15, 1960, p. 5.

23. Greg Bautzer, interview, May 5, 1972.

24. It is not clear how much Wilkerson paid Sedway, nor if he continued to retain Sedway and Greenbaum's services in the casino operation. Title and deed of land transfer were executed and recorded on November 11, 1945 in Clark County, Nevada

(Book 40 of Deeds, p. 382).

25. Greg Bautzer, interview, May 5, 1972.

26-27. Ibid. Thomas F. Seward, interview, December 15, 1992.

28-29. George H. Kennedy, Jr., interview, December 24, 1987.

30. Ibid. Jennings, We Only Kill Each Other, p. 152.

31-32. George H. Kennedy, Jr., interview, December 24, 1987. According to Kennedy, Tom Seward, Wilkerson's business partner, paid everyone off in cash for the publisher before closing down the project.

33. Rothberg made his approach to the publisher in early February 1946 and remained involved until the finalizing of the deal. After the agreement was signed he vanished and did not reappear again until after Ben Siegel's death in June 1947.

34. Lowell Bergman, interview, July 23, 1992.

35. Messick, Secret File, p. 206.

36-41. Greg Bautzer, interview, May 5, 1972.

42. Nevada Project Corporation Document, Release of All Demands, March 19, 1947.

43. Greg Bautzer, interview, May 5, 1972. Although some believe that Wilkerson received his funding to complete the Flamingo in July 1946, after the El Cortez syndicate had divested itself of the hotel, he was in fact funded by the consortium much earlier, around the beginning of March.

44. Ibid.

7. THE INVESTORS

1. CLOSE-UP, September 13, 1962, p. 5. TIME, July 3, 1945, p. 76. Murphy, George. "Say... Didn't You Used To Be George Murphy?" p. 52.

2. TIME, July 3, 1944, p. 76.

3. Mobsters Willie Bioff and George Browne orchestrated general strikes in Hollywood during the mid 1940s successfully extorting money from the industry's hierarchy. Their muscle and backing came from one of the large unions in town, the

International Alliance of Theatrical Stage Employees (I.A.T.S.E.) which they controlled at the time.
4. TIME, July 3, 1944, p. 76.
5. Edith Gwynn, interview, August 1972.
6. Harry Drucker, interview, July 18, 1983. Tom Seward, interview, December 15, 1992.
7. Giesler, The Jerry Giesler Story, p. 237-8.
8. Ibid., p. 239.
9. Patrick Jenning and Marshall Croddy, interview, September 2, 1993.
10. George H. Kennedy, Jr., interview, August 1972.
11-13. Ibid.
14. Greg Bautzer, interview, May 5, 1972.
15. Harry Drucker, interview, July 18, 1983.
16. George H. Kennedy, Jr., interview, August 1972.
17. Beatrice Sedway, interview, May 23, 1992.
18. Greg Bautzer, interview, May 5, 1972.
19. Ibid.
20. George H. Kennedy, Jr., interview, August 1972.
21. Ibid.
22. Kate Stadelman, interview, July 23, 1992.
23. George H. Kennedy, Jr., interview, August 1972.
24-25. Ibid.

8. THE HOTEL

1. Greg Bautzer, interview, May 5, 1972. It has long been thought that Siegel was involved in the Flamingo as early as mid-1945. His name, however, does not appear on any documentation prior to February 1946. A fruitless search was also made for all Nevada Project Corporation documents.
2. George H. Kennedy, Jr., interview, August 1972.
3. Greg Bautzer, interview, May 5, 1972.
4. George H. Kennedy, Jr., interview, August 1972.
5-6. Ibid.

7. Greg Bautzer, interview, May 5, 1972.

8. Thomas F. Seward, interview, December 15, 1992.

9. Ibid.

10. George H. Kennedy, Jr., interview, August 1972.

11. Ibid.

12. Thomas F. Seward, interview, December 15, 1992.

13. George H. Kennedy, Jr., interview, August 1972.

14. Colin Russell, interview, September 1, 1992.

15. Greg Bautzer, interview, May 5, 1972.

16. George H. Kennedy, Jr., interview, August 1972.

17. Thomas F. Seward, interview, August 1972.

18. George H. Kennedy, Jr., interview, August 1972.

19-23. Ibid. According to Kennedy, whenever his employer was asked about Siegel's role in the project, the publisher described the gangster as a silent investor and a "helping hand." Unsatisfied with this answer, star syndicated newspaper columnist Westbrook Pegler approached Siegel directly and asked him to describe Wilkerson's precise involvement in the project. He received the terse reply quoted.

24. Greg Bautzer, interview, May 5, 1972. According to Bautzer and Kennedy, Johnny Rosselli and Moe Dalitz, both personal friends of the publisher, imparted this information to Wilkerson some years after the gangster's death. Each had strong links to organized crime and criminal activities. No documentation or correspondence exists to confirm where or when they met. Wilkerson relayed their story to Bautzer and Kennedy at a later date.

25-26. Ibid.

27. George H. Kennedy, Jr., interview, August 1972.

28. Greg Bautzer, interview, May 5, 1972.

29. Investigative Reporters and Editors, Inc., 1977, The Arizona Project, p. 15. Records in Clark Country, Nevada show Del E. Webb was hired by Billy Wilkerson and Gus Greenbaum.

30. Greg Bautzer, interview, May 5, 1972.

31-32. Ibid.

33. George H. Kennedy, Jr., interview, August 1972.

9. THE NEVADA PROJECT

1. The law firm which handled the incorporation of the Nevada Project Corporation was Pacht, Elton, Warne, Ross & Bernhard in Los Angeles. Articles of Incorporation for the Nevada Project reside in Sacramento, California.

2. Greg Bautzer, interview, May 5, 1972.

3. Ibid.

4. George H. Kennedy, Jr., interview, August 1972.

5. Ibid.

6. Greg Bautzer, interview, May 5, 1972.

7. Jennings, p. 152.

8. Louis Wiener, interview, April 22, 1993.

9. Greg Bautzer, interview, May 5, 1972.

10-12. Ibid.

13. George H. Kennedy, Jr., interview, August 1972.

14. Kate Stadelman, interview, July 27, 1992.

15. Jennings, p. 152

16. Greg Bautzer, interview, May 5, 1972.

17. Jennings, p. 176. Nevada Project Corporation account, check No. 1384 for $50,000.

18. Investigative Reporters and Editors, Inc., 1977, The Arizona Project, p. 15. Webb eventually exacted payment from Siegel. Bautzer recalled that he was at the same meeting with Webb and that the contractor "settled for part cash and part stock."

19. Tichi Kassel, interview, August 21, 1991.

20. George H. Kennedy, Jr., interview, August 1972.

21. The first parcel of property, still under attorney Greg Bautzer's name, was quitclaimed and deeded to the Nevada Project Corporation on July 31, 1946.

22. George H. Kennedy, Jr., interview, August 1972.

23. Wilkerson quitclaimed and deeded his final parcel of land to the Nevada Project Corporation on November 27, 1946.

24. Greg Bautzer, interview, May 5, 1972. According to Bautzer, Gus Greenbaum tipped Wilkerson off that the true figure spent

to date on the Flamingo was close to $4.5 million. By December 26, 1946, the Flamingo was advertised as costing over $5 million.

25. George H. Kennedy, Jr., interview, August 1972.

26. By early December 1946, Wilkerson had accumulated 48 percent of over $5 million.

27. George H. Kennedy, Jr., interview, August 1972.

28. Ibid.

29. Greg Bautzer, interview, May 5, 1972.

30-31. Ibid.

32. George H. Kennedy, Jr., interview, August 1972.

33-36. Ibid.

10. THE MEETING

1. George H. Kennedy, Jr. interview, August 1972.

2. An FBI search conducted in 1992 revealed a surprisingly small file for such a notable high-profile figure as Wilkerson. Hoover's fondness for the publisher may well have influenced the number of entries into his personal file.

3. George H. Kennedy, Jr. interview, August 1972.

4. Vic Enyart, interview, December 1980.

5. Ibid.

6. Greg Bautzer, interview, May 5, 1972.

7. Jennings, p. 173. Syndicated columnist Westbrook Pegler had routinely referred to Siegel and his cohorts as "a group of henchmen carpetbaggers." During an interview, Wilkerson told Pegler the FBI director had personally phoned him to warn that he was associated with "the worst bunch of gangsters in the underworld."

8. Jennings, p. 156.

9. Greg Bautzer, interview, May 5, 1972. Although Wiener and Jones do not recall being present at the meeting, Bautzer was absolutely positive that they were in attendance.

10. Investigative Reporters and Editors, Inc., 1977, The Arizona Project, p. 15.

11. Greg Bautzer, interview, May 5, 1972.
12. Ibid. This is Bautzer's own memory and paraphrasing of what occurred and what was said at the meeting. The author was unable to locate copies of the affidavits described at the meeting. The exact date and time of the meeting is unknown.
13. Greg Bautzer, interview, May 5, 1972. Bautzer's own memory in the interview.
14. George H. Kennedy, Jr., interview, August 1972.
15-17. Greg Bautzer, interview, May 5, 1972.

11. PARIS

1. Greg Bautzer, interview, May 5, 1972. This was done on Bautzer's advice.
2. George H. Kennedy, Jr., interview, August 1972.
3. Greg Bautzer, interview, May 5, 1972.
4. Ibid. Believing Siegel had gone too far, Wilkerson briefly toyed with the idea of circumventing Siegel and his attorneys by contacting Moe Sedway directly. But soon after his departure for Paris, Sedway mysteriously disappeared from the project altogether.
5. The ads appeared in The Hollywood Reporter, Friday, December 27, 1946, the day after the formal gala opening of the Flamingo.
6. Nobody from Wilkerson's camp, attorney Greg Bautzer, general manager George Kennedy nor business partner Thomas Seward, attended the opening.
7. Thomas F. Seward, interview, December 15, 1992.
8. Ibid. According to Seward, Hughes himself also volunteered to fly a few hand-picked celebrities including Wilkerson and himself, to the opening in his converted B-25. But at the last moment Hughes was called away to Washington Senate hearings concerning his use of government funding for military activities during WW II. When he could not make it to the Las Vegas opening, Hughes sent both Wilkerson and his partner, Tom

Seward, gold Piaget watches.

9. George H. Kennedy, Jr., interview, August 1972.

10-13. Ibid. David Alexander interview, August 1972.

14. George H. Kennedy, Jr., interview, August 1972.

15. Ibid.

16. There has been some dispute over the Flamingo's true cost. While it is likely never to be known, Greg Bautzer, Thomas F. Seward and George H. Kennedy, Jr., all agree on the $6 million price tag. The hotel was advertised at costing over $5 million in the Friday, December 27, 1946 issue of The Hollywood Reporter. Factoring in Wilkerson's initial investment brings the total close to $6.6 million.

17. Greg Bautzer, interview, May 5, 1972.

18. Ibid.

19. Thomas F. Seward, interview, December 15, 1992.

20. Ibid.

21. Siegel's Los Angeles attorney, N. Joseph Ross of the law firm Pacht, Elton, Warne, Ross & Bernhard in Beverly Hills, drew up the Release of All Demands.

22. George H. Kennedy, Jr., interview, August 1972.

23. Tichi Kassel, interview, August 21, 1991.

24. George H. Kennedy, Jr., interview, August 1972.

25. Greg Bautzer, interview, May 5, 1972.

26. Thomas F. Seward, interview, December 15, 1992.

27. Tradeview, The Hollywood Reporter, June 3, 1947.

28. Another theory is that the syndicate had had enough of the gangster and set him up to fail by demanding that he re-coup all the massive cost overruns he had by an impossible deadline (April 1, 1947).

29. Greg Bautzer, interview, May 5, 1972.

30. George H. Kennedy, Jr., interview, August 1972. George Kennedy and Greg Bautzer were clear that the warning came by phone. Kennedy believed that Moe Dalitz and Johnny Rosselli, who had a fondness for his employer and a dislike of Siegel, may have been looking out for Wilkerson. Kennedy strongly suggested the possibility that either man, sympathetic to the publisher's

plight, could have sent him the warning. During his New York speakeasy days, Wilkerson received frequent warnings of impending police raids from friends and associates in organized crime.

31. Ibid.

32. Wilkerson was also in Paris at the same time as Virginia Hill. There is a theory that Siegel heard that Wilkerson was hiding in Paris and sent Hill there to locate his exact whereabouts so that he could call in a hit. Alternatively, it is possible that, knowing how Siegel's partners operated, Hill took steps to avoid being in the same room with Siegel at a time he was in trouble. The street-savvy Hill knew that if Siegel was marked for death, the hitman would not hesitate to eliminate her at the same time. Knowing this and fearing for her own life, it makes sense that she followed Wilkerson's example and fled the country.

33. George H. Kennedy, Jr., interview, August 1972.

12. THE END

1. Beatrice Sedway, interview, May 23, 1992. Moe's widow hinted that, although she knew the reason why Siegel died and who was behind his slaying, she was not saying. It is possible that her unwillingness to reveal this information is based on the lack of a statute of limitations on murder and her fears of being linked as an accessory or accomplice to the crime.

2. Greg Bautzer, interview, May 5, 1972.

3. Ibid.

4. George H. Kennedy, Jr., interview, August 1972.

5. Ibid.

6. Wilkerson correspondence. The journey took place on Tuesday, January 17, 1950.

7. Tichi Kassel, interview, August 21, 1991.

8. Howard Hawks, interview, August 1972.

9. Greg Bautzer, interview, May 5, 1972.

Appendices

Appendix A:
Chronology of Events

Mid-February, 1945 – Wilkerson purchases 33 acres of land outside the town of Las Vegas for $84,000.

June, 1945 – Wilkerson leases the El Rancho Vegas from owner Joe Drown for six months.

September 2nd, 1945 – World War II ends in the Pacific.

Late-November, 1945 – Building and construction begins on the Flamingo Hotel.

February 26, 1946 – Wilkerson signs first agreement with G. Harry Rothberg for funding to complete his project.

June 20, 1946 – Ben Siegel forms the Nevada Project Corporation of California.

June 26, 1946 – Ben Siegel buys first parcel of Wilkerson's Flamingo land.

August 22, 1946 – Ben Siegel buys remaining parcel of Wilkerson's Flamingo land.

Early-December, 1946 – Ben Siegel threatens Wilkerson's life. Wilkerson leaves the country and hides out in Paris.

December 26, 1946 – Ben Siegel opens the Flamingo Hotel.

Late-January, 1947 – Ben Siegel shuts down the hotel.

March 1, 1947 – Ben Siegel reopens the hotel.

March 19, 1947 – Wilkerson receives Release of All Demands from Nevada Project Corporation and Ben

Siegel.

Mid-April, 1947 – Wilkerson sells his interest in the Flamingo Hotel to the Nevada Project Corporation.

June 20, 1947 – Siegel is shot dead.

June 23, 1947 – Wilkerson returns to California from Paris.

Tuesday, January 17, 1950 – Wilkerson arrives in Sun Valley, Idaho with his fiancee. A few days later he is confronted by Virginia Hill, Siegel's longtime girlfriend.

Appendix B:
Documentation

Sometime in 1951, Wilkerson systematically destroyed all his documentation covering the period from 1930 – 1950. These documents had been subpoenaed as evidence in a lawsuit brought by Wilkerson's ex-partner Tom Seward. Rather than risk losing half his business to Seward, Wilkerson chose to torch any and all incriminating evidence. The publisher was almost cited for destroying evidence but, as usual, powerful business and political connections came to his aid.

Wilkerson's general manager, George H. Kennedy, Jr., managed to keep certain important documents out of the office bonfire. One which escaped the flames was the Release of All Demands. This Nevada Project document, bearing Siegel's name and signature, guaranteed Wilkerson's release from the corporation.

The following letter from George Kennedy to the author explains what happened to Wilkerson's documentation in more detail.

> 17 October, 1981
> Ramona, CA 92065
> Dear Scout:
> A throw-away line of yours while you were still at the task of recovering memorabilia of your father's in my files, foot locker, etc., etc., gnawed at me thru two nights. Then, early this morning, regressive memory restored an answer and explanation.
> Do you recall, you said something to the effect there was a lacuna of some years of any information?
> I woke with a start early this morning and remembered why that was:
> At the time TFS (Thomas F. Seward), your father's own outside accountant, and others, were trying to claim ownership for Tom of more of the paper than your father had granted him — at the bad and venal advice of the accountant: that

giving away a certain percentage of the paper would yield your father greater income, etc., etc., — the lawsuit came about. They wanted to subpoena all files, records, correspondence, etc., etc., for the time antedate to his consent to grant a minority share of the paper to Seward, for the time thereafter up to when your father discovered how much bigger a slice of the pie they cut for him than your father wanted.

When we learned this, your father and I had a bonfire in his office fireplace three days running, burning correspondence, bookkeeping records, tax receipts, etc. So much so, one day there was a flue fire and the fire department came trooping up the stairs outside your father's office. But for the good graces of Harry Brand, we would have been cited, and in real legal trouble. But it all past over.

That's the story, the whole story, so help me Hannah!

Love,

George

Appendix C:
Las Vegas Hotels & Casinos

(circa 1946)

HOTELS

Apache Hotel
El Cortez Hotel
Nevada Biltmore Hotel
Last Frontier Hotel
El Rancho Vegas Hotel
MacDonald Hotel
El Patio Hotel
Charleston Hotel
Kit Carson Hotel
El Playtel Motel
Lake Mead Lodge (in
Boulder)
Boulder Dam Hotel (in
Boulder)

CASINOS

Pioneer Club
Golden Nugget Club
Boulder Club
Frontier Club
Eldorado Club
El Toro Club
Players Club
Red Rooster Club
Savoy Club
Kit Carson Casino
Pair-O-Dice Club (91 Club)
S. S. Rex Club
Monte Carlo Club
Las Vegas Club
Casa Vegas Club

Source: The Hollywood Reporter, Friday, December 27, 1946

Appendix D:
The Flamingo's Principal Contractors

Decorator, *Tom Douglas.*

Architect for Casino, Restaurant, Shops, Swimming Pool and Future Cottages, *George Vernon Russell.*

Landscaping, Pool and all Outdoor Facilities, *Eduardo Jose Samaniego.*

General Contractor for Billy Wilkerson, *Bud Raulston.*

Architect for the Hotel, *Richard R. Stadelman.*

General Contractor for Ben Siegel, *Del E. Webb.*

Painting Contractors, *Klaas Brothers.*

Plastering Contractors, *Carroll Duncan & Co.*

Drilling, *Canemona Drilling Company.*

Excavating, Grading, Asphalt, *V. W. Graham Construction Co.*

General Contractors for Paving, Excavations, Land Clearing, Leveling, Plowing, Posthole Digging, *Kauffman and Jensen, Inc.*

Millwork, *Walter R. Cluer.*

Ready-Mixed Concrete and Pumice Block Materials, *Las Vegas Building Materials.*

Suppliers of Lumber, Millwork, Building Materials, Hardware and Paints, *Opaco Lumber.*

Suppliers of Lumber, *Ed Von Tobel Lumber Co.*

Suppliers of Rock and Gravel, *Purdy's Gravel and Block Plant.*

Plumbing and Heating, *A. R. Ruppert Co.*

Hotel Furnishings and Club Equipment, *Albert Parvin Co.*

All Lighting Displays and Sound Equipment, *Otto K. Olesen Co.*

Installation of all Electrical Power, Lighting and Lighting Effects, *Bennett-Forsberg Electric Co.*

Restaurant and Institutional Foods and Supplies, *Ross Supply Co.*

Commercial Refrigeration, *Super Cold Products.*
Suppliers of Poultry, *Southern California Poultry Co.*
Distributors of Meat, *Steven's Market Co.*
Suppliers of Fine Meats, *Davidson Meat Co.*
Suppliers of Produce, *G & G Produce Co.*
Imported and Domestic Groceries, *Ostroff Trading Co.*
Distributors of Fine Liquors, Wine, Beer and Beverages,
    Las Vegas Distributing Company.
Suppliers of Beverages, *Nevada Beverage Company.*

Source: The Hollywood Reporter, Friday, December 27, 1946

Appendix E:
The Flamingo's Investors

There were twenty-two original investors in the Nevada Project Corporation, the company behind the Flamingo Hotel. Below is a partial list of the key shareholders. It is not known exactly how many were part of the eastern syndicate. This list does not include those later investors who bought stock from Siegel when he was attempting to raise additional funding.

Hyman Abrahams
Willie Alderman
Davie Berman
Gus Greenbaum
Meyer Lansky
Louis Pokross
Morris Rosen
N. Joseph Ross
G. Harry Rothberg
Samuel Rothberg
Moe Sedway
Benjamin Siegel
Charles L. Straus
Billy Wilkerson

Source: Greg Bautzer

Appendix F:
Wilkerson's letter to Moe Sedway

Tuesday.
Mr. Moe Sedway
El Cortez Hotel,
Las Vegas, Nev.

My dear Moe:

I have become convinced that Las Vegas is too dangerous for me. I have had this thought for months and each
time I would go up was with the determination of doing a
little gambling for the pleasure I could get, but would
always end with ten or twelve hours of it – and generally
with bad financial results. Am afraid that should I go in
business up there I would be another Chickie Berman. I
like gambling too much, like to shoot craps and drive
myself nuts and the only way I can defeat it is to keep away
from any place that has it. And that what I'm going to do.

This decision should not, in any way, influence Gus and
yourself from going though with the project as it is a certain big winner and no one could accomplish it any better
than you two. I think too that you should use the layout I
had drawn up because it is rich, sufficiently big and could
be built economically and when opened, few if any would
try to create something in opposition to you. Let the others
build their hotels, let them have that headache, you should
stick to this because anyone, venturing on any building up
there, particularly hotels, will do so with only one purpose,
to try and attract patrons for their casino's. You don't need
a hotel for that with the layout I have suggested, you will
take people away from the hotels and you will not be burdened, nor have your casino burdened with a hotel, its ser-

vice and its expense both of building and operation.

I left rather hurriedly, first because they stepped up the departure of my plane from 11:15 to 9:00 P.M. and secondly I was so disgusted with myself for losing [almost $10,000] that I was mad and wanted to get away. I owe you $5,000 which I wish you would deduct from the $9,000 I have in the Folsum property, together with the $500 for the set of first drawings for the project. I would like for you to handle the thing in this manner as I'm a bit short of cash inasmuch as I have over $60,000 worth of printing equipment landing here this week which I wish to pay cash for instead of financing it and paying interest. If there is any objection, let me know.

I want you to know that I will be happy to be of any service, that will not take me to Las Vegas, in the building, operation or planning of the idea we started. I can be of much help to you here in talent, in seeing that you get a good crew for your dining room and kitchen and other things what I would be delighted to do.

It's my impression that you will be much better off without me, inasmuch as there are so many others you have to declare in, which will place some of the burden on those for construction and operation that would have otherwise been on our shoulders.

Let me hear from you and give my best to Gus.
Sincerely,

Billy Wilkerson

Source: This letter comes from the archives of Beatrice Sedway, widow of Moe Sedway.

The letter is undated, but Wilkerson's "customer's" checks allow this gambling binge to be dated between July 13 & 14, 1945, some seven months before Siegel was in the picture.

PARAGRAPH ONE:

"I have become convinced that Las Vegas is too dangerous for me."

Beatrice Sedway, Moe's widow, has interpreted this phrase to mean that Wilkerson feared for his life. She guessed that he was being threatened by Siegel and his partners. Greg Bautzer, Wilkerson's attorney, maintained however, that Sedway's connections were of no particular consequence to the publisher. Wilkerson's only concern was the successful outcome of the project. It was only later, after Siegel's arrival and the subsequent threats against his life that misgivings arose.

Viewed in this light, Wilkerson is clearly referring to his recurrent fear of bankrupting himself through uncontrolled gambling. Las Vegas was "too dangerous" for his wallet. Losing close to $10,000 in July proved to be the final straw. In a wildly impulsive, but entirely characteristic decision, the publisher threw in the towel on the Flamingo project. Vegas was no longer for him.

It was not unusual for Wilkerson to have second thoughts about a project and throw in the towel. George Kennedy reported that on several occasions, such do-or-die soul-searching plagued the publisher for weeks. Even Bautzer mentioned how Wilkerson agonized over the Rothberg deal. In the late 1950s, on a similar whim, he even put his beloved Hollywood Reporter up for sale (to Walter Annenberg). But the Flamingo, like so many of his good ideas was resurrected from the waste-paper basket at a later date.

"Am afraid that should I go in business up there I would be another Chickie Berman."

Chickie Berman was the brother of Davie Berman, one of the prominent partners in the Flamingo after the death of Ben Siegel. The Berman brothers had been gangsters in Minneapolis. Their life is well described in Susan Berman's book Easy Street. Susan is Davie's daughter and describes her uncle Chickie as a hopeless gambler, forever getting into debt and turning to his brother for money. He outlived Davie and died destitute.

PARAGRAPH TWO:

He encourages Moe Sedway and Gus Greenbaum to carry on without him. Although there were plans for a hotel (initially, there were two separate sets of drawings – one that included a hotel, and one that did not), as a direct result of the disgust he felt over this current gambling debt it is interesting to note that he doubted this idea. In the end, he chose to relinquish the entire project rather than remain involved with anything that would encourage his destructive habit.

Ironically the two men did not carry on after Wilkerson's departure. After buying back the land from Sedway, Wilkerson began building in late November 1945. It was only after he ran out of funds in late January 1946 that he partnered with Rothberg who brought Siegel into the venture in February.

PARAGRAPH THREE:

At some point there was joint ownership between Sedway and Wilkerson in the Folsom Property. To what extent is not known, even by Beatrice Sedway. Excluding this single reference, there is a complete lack of documentation, legal or otherwise, indicating any type of partnership between them. However, in the odd mechanics of debt settlement described in this letter, Wilkerson, who still owed money to Sedway in September 1945, deeded the land to him until he could raise the cash to pay the debt.

PARAGRAPH FOUR:

"...in the building, operation or planning of the idea we started."

Here Wilkerson gives the two men shared credit for the project. Greenbaum and Sedway could, of course, have chosen to act on such an idea (had it occurred to them) long before they met Wilkerson. Instead they bought into the El Cortez in December 1945. But the letter does reveal that Wilkerson was talking with them from the start.

Wilkerson had a habit of making partners out of key employees and consultants. For example, he often made his restaurant cooks into silent partners, considered them family members and treated them as equals. It was his practice to hire, and then partner with the very best professionals money could buy at the onset of any project. By making these key people silent partners, he guaranteed their loyalty to the venture. They would be much less likely to listen to competing offers and leave him in the lurch.

Wilkerson partnered with Sedway and Greenbaum for the same reason. He saw the success they had created at the El Cortez, befriended the two men and asked for their help. Initially, they acted as consultants in casino management. While the publisher was fluent in every aspect of fine dining and entertainment shows, his knowledge of the managerial workings that went into a casino operation of any size, was limited. The publisher needed the skills these two men possessed so he eventually made them his partners.

Exactly how and when the publisher met Greenbaum and Sedway remains a mystery. It is highly probable that he first made their acquaintance at the El Cortez. As a "high roller," Wilkerson gambled heavily and frequently all over Las Vegas. Dropping tens of thousands of dollars at a sitting made him highly visible to casino owners and operators. Many gave him extraordinary lines of gambling credit knowing his sterling reputation for honoring his gambling debts.

One of the most striking things about this letter is the intimacy of its tone. By nature, Wilkerson was a private man, not prone to disclosing his vulnerabilities in business letters. That he should write to Sedway and Greenbaum in such self-revealing phrases denotes the closeness of their relationship.

This letter also serves as an astounding testament to the depths of Wilkerson's addiction. These are the words of a defeated man who knows he has lost his struggle for self-control. They illuminate two important aspects of the publisher's character: one, that he was indeed a chronic gambler prone to losing staggering amounts, and two, that he was plagued by the emotional costs of this disorder. These pages then can be read as a confession; confirming and highlighting Wilkerson's continuing struggle to master his compulsion. We can also detect the typical reaction of any addict – blatant self-disgust after a night of over-indulgence. This is similar, for example, to the dieter who, having binged-out the evening before, resolves not to eat at all upon awakening the next morning.

Books

Berman, Susan. *Easy Street*. New York: Dial Press, 1981.

Birmingham, Stephen. *The Rest of Us*. Boston: Little, Brown, 1984.

Edmonds, Andy. *Bugsy's Baby: The Secret Life of Mob Queen Virginia Hill*. New York: Birch Lane Press, 1993.

Finch, Christopher & Linda Rosenkrantz, *Gone Hollywood: The Movie Colony In the Golden Age*. New York: Doubleday & Company, 1979.

Fredrich, Otto. *City of Nets*. New York: Perennial Library, 1987.

Giegsler, Jerry and Pete Martin. *The Jerry Giesler Story*. New York: Simon & Schuster, 1960.

Hess, Alan. *Viva Las Vegas: After-Hours Architecture*. San Francisco: Chronicle Books, 1993.

Investigative Reporters and Editors, Inc. *The Arizona Project*. 1977.

Jennings, Dean. *We Only Kill Each Other: The Life and Bad Times of Bugsy Siegel*. New York: Pocket Books, January, 1992.

Lacey, Robert. *Little Man: Meyer Lansky and the Gangster*

Life. Boston: Little, Brown and Co., 1991.

Messick, Hank. *Secret File*. New York: G. P. Putnam's Sons, 1969.

Moehring, Eugene P., *Resort City in the Sunbelt: Las Vegas, 1930-1970*. Nevada: University of Nevada Press, 1989.

Murphy, George, with Victor Lasky. *Say...Din't You Use To Be George Murphy?* New York: Bartholomew House, Ltd.: July, 1970.

Pileggi, Nicholas. *Casino: Love and Honor in Las Vegas*. New York: Simon & Schuster, 1995.

Reid, Ed & Ovid Demaris. *The Green Felt Jungle*. London: Cox & Wyman, 1965.

Rappleye, Charles and Ed Becker. *All American Mafioso: The Johnny Roselli Story*. New York: Doubleday, 1991.

Turner, Wallace. *Gambler's Money*. Boston: Houghton Mifflin, 1965.

Wilkerson, Tichi, and Marcia Borie. *The Hollywood Reporter*. New York: Coward-McCan, 1983.

Zion, Sidney. *Loyalty and Betrayal: The Story of the American Mob*. Collins Publishers, 1994.

Newspaper & Magazine Articles

Dutka, Elaine. "A Mobster's Neon Dream". *Los Angeles Times*. July 14, 1991.

Stein, Herb. "Inside Hollywood". *Racing Form*. September 8, 1962.

Pegler, Westbrook. As Pegler Sees It – "'Bugsy' Siegel's Friends". *King Features Syndicate*, Inc. 1957.

Collins, Roscoe. "George Raft's Gangster Friend". *Salute*, May 1947.

Acknowledgements

There were those who would not discuss Billy Wilkerson with me. Their silence only increases my gratitude to the many who did. My deepest thanks go to all those who gave so graciously of their time and energy, in particular: Natalie Bazarevitsch, Lowell Bergman, Bettye Binder, Andrew Craissoti, Mr. and Mrs. Donald O'Connor, Carol Cornell, Will Doheny, Harry Drucker, Jack & Scott Enyart, Herb McDonald, Bill Feeder, Murray Fields, Brownie Franson, Hugh John Gibson, Peggy Hammerschmidt, Alan Hess, Susan Jarvis, Cliff A. Jones, Tichi Kassel, Howard Kotch Sr., Donn Knepp, Neva Mason, Charles Rappleye, Colin Russell, Bee Sedway, Kate Stadelman, Vivian Wilhite and Frank Wright.

People past: David Alexander, Greg Bautzer, Marcia Borie, Cubby Broccoli, Vic Enyart, Edith Gwynn, Howard Hawks, Norman Krasna, George H. Kennedy, Jr., "Junior" Laemmle, Joe Pasternak, Joe Rivkin, Howard Strickling, Lana Turner, Raoul Walsh, and Louis Wiener.

The media: Art Durbano, Denny Arar of *The Daily News*, Kenneth Turan and Sharon Bernstein of *The Los Angeles Times*, Bob Shemeligian of *The Las Vegas Sun*.

Special thanks: Thomas F. Seward, my father's business

partner for more than a decade. Hollywood historians, Pat Jenning and Marshall Croddy for hours of insightful assistance. Armen Tavitian for his excellent cover art and production work. Shelley Hubbard, Howard and Karen at Brooks Howard for overseeing the entire book production process. Claudette Powell-Hume for her meticulous proofreading. Lastly, I would like to remember Ronnie Baron and Dick Weaver who inspired me to finally write this book.

This book, however, would not have been possible at all without the invaluable help and support of three individuals.

First, to my good friend and publicist, Elizabeth Caulder, for her friendship and support throughout the years.

The second is my friend and co-conspirator, British filmmaker and writer, Daniel W. Gilbertson, who edited my thoughts and words, ensuring that my father's story rose from the page into vivid life.

Last, but not least, a heartfelt thanks to British biographer and historian, Robert Lacey. It was Robert who, in *Little Man* (1991), published the first accurate account of the Flamingo Hotel, citing Wilkerson as the resort's originator. Throughout the long writing process, he has been a wonderful mentor, teacher and friend, who painstakingly edited the manuscript twice for historical inaccuracies.

Credits

Elizabeth Caulder, *publicity*
Armen Tavitian, *book design & production manager*
Daniel W. Gilbertson, *editor*
Robert Lacey, *historical editor*
Claudette Powell-Hume, *proofreading*
Micki Taylor, *indexing*
Shelley Hubbard, *book design and layout*
Susan Karasic, *layout*

Further Information

For additional copies of this book please send a check or money order for $17.00 plus $5.00 s&h ($7.00 foreign orders) to:

CIRO'S BOOKS
PMB 1352
270 North Canon Drive
Beverly Hills, CA 90210

Please allow 4 to 6 weeks for delivery.

For more information on this subject and the early history of
Las Vegas, please contact:
The Nevada State Museum
(702) 486-5205

PUBLICITY
Elizabeth Caulder & Associates
(310) 456-2076

About The Author

W. R. Wilkerson III is a free-lance writer who was raised and educated in England. He has been a contributor to numerous newspapers and periodicals, including *The Los Angeles Times*, *The Hollywood Reporter*, *USA Today*, *The Herald Examiner* and *The LA Weekly*. Wilkerson resides in Los Angeles.

Index

In subheadings, W.R. "Billy" Wilkerson is referred to as "WRW."

Index

Index

Index